Jersey Shore
FOOD HISTORY

Jersey Shore
FOOD HISTORY
Victorian Feasts to Boardwalk Treats

KAREN L. SCHNITZSPAHN
Foreword by Margaret Thomas Buchholz

AMERICAN PALATE

Published by American Palate
A Division of The History Press
Charleston, SC 29403
www.historypress.net

Cover images: Front: top courtesy of Ollie Klein's Fish Market, Belmar; bottom right courtesy of Kohr's Frozen Custard Inc., Seaside Park; bottom left courtesy of Bahrs Landing, Highlands. Back: bottom photo of Jack Bahrs and waitresses courtesy of Bahrs Landing, Highlands.

All images courtesy of author unless otherwise noted.

First published 2012

Manufactured in the United States

ISBN 978.1.60949.507.7

Library of Congress CIP data applied for.

Notice: The information in this book is true and complete to the best of our knowledge. It is offered without guarantee on the part of the author or The History Press. The author and The History Press disclaim all liability in connection with the use of this book.

In memory of my dear friend and mentor,
the distinguished New Jersey author and historian,
George H. Moss Jr. (1923–2009)

Contents

Foreword

As I read Karen L. Schnitzspahn's book about the history of food on the Jersey Shore, I thought about my childhood at the edge of the sea, redolent of crabs and clams from the bay outside my window and fresh striped bass and bluefish from the ocean two blocks away. Until I was an adult, however, this succulent local seafood never passed my lips. Clams were for digging and crabs were for netting, to be sold to the local clam bar—every town along the shore had one. We sometimes had fish on Fridays, but my father had a brief, unsuccessful foray as a fisherman, and he didn't want to see anything with scales on his dinner plate.

Tourists were a different kettle of fish. They came to the shore especially to eat the bounty from the sea. *Jersey Shore Food History: Victorian Feasts to Boardwalk Treats* takes us back to a time when vacationers came by stagecoach, then by train and finally (in the twentieth century) by car, anticipating the seafood and local produce as an important part of their summer holiday. They came first to boardinghouses and then to huge, oceanfront hotels, where their dinner plates were loaded, truly loaded, with seafood and everything else.

This excursion throughout the Jersey Shore's culinary and restaurant history takes us from the 1850s, when oysters were plentiful and visitors were introduced to the produce that made New Jersey the Garden State—squash, tomatoes and sweet, succulent corn—to the mid-twentieth century's pizza, salt water taffy, subs and hot dogs. The author's insightful research brings us stories of what people ate and where they dined, from white tablecloth restaurants to boardwalk food stands. And it is packed with lavish illustrations and recipes to tempt us into the kitchen.

I first met Karen at a Monmouth County history fair. She has documented that county's history in a number of books. Her first book (with mentor George H. Moss Jr.), *Those Innocent Years*, has a proud place in my New Jersey library, and I am especially impressed with *The Roaring '20s at the Jersey Shore*, a sumptuous feast of text and images, bringing the period to life. Now she takes us on a delicious, meandering journey from Sandy Hook to Cape May, with side tours to inland farms.

It's a wonderfully tasty trip.

—Margaret Thomas Buchholz

Margaret is author, editor or co-author of books, including Great Storms of the Jersey Shore, New Jersey Shipwrecks, Shore Chronicles *and* Josephine: From Washington Working Girl to Fisherman's Wife.

Acknowledgements

T his work could not have been possible without the help and encouragement of so many incredible people. Each one contributed in some unique way. I'm grateful to Lynne Olver, editor of the Food Timeline website (foodtimeline.org), for reading the manuscript and for her suggestions. Sincere thanks go to author Margaret Thomas Buchholz for writing the foreword. I appreciate my friend and colleague Sandra Epstein for her assistance (our research jaunts are always fun!). Thank you to Chef Brian Gualtieri, owner of the Piccola Italia in Ocean, New Jersey, for his input. I am indebted to fellow authors Vicki Gold Levi, Anita Hirsch and Randall Gabrielan and artist Marie Natale for their contributions. Special thanks to Bonita Craft Grant of Rutgers Alexander Library, Doug Oxenhorn of the New Jersey Historical Society and Albertine Senske of the Whitesbog Preservation Trust. Thank you to George Crumbler of Taylor Provisions, Sue Laudeman of the Lobster House, Lisa Glaser Whitley of James Candy Company, Allen Boo Pergament (and in memory of his wife, Marlene), Jane Eigenrauch, Donald H. Dewey, Don Burden, Anthony Kutshera, Jack Sinn and food historian Judith Krall Russo.

Thank you to Becky Cosgrove of Bahrs Landing, Peter Cancro of Jersey Mike's, Frank Dougherty and Chef Michael Newkirk of the Knife and Fork Inn, John Stauffer of Johnson's Popcorn, Jennifer and Michele Maybaum of Max's Famous Hot Dogs, Chris Walton of Pete & Elda's, Joe Maruca of Maruca's Tomato Pies, Tom Grieg of Case's Pork Roll, Mike Corrigan of Kohr's The Original, Bruce Kohr of Kohr's Frozen Custard Inc., Kevin

McCarty of the Renault Winery, Mark A. Brockriede of Monmouth Enterprises, Eric Greenberg of Cape Resorts Group, Jennifer O'Connor of Sickles Market, Karen Irvine, Jim Filip of Doris & Ed's and Doug Doughty of the Lusty Lobster. Thanks to the Township of Ocean Historical Society, the Point Pleasant Historical Society, the Shrewsbury Historical Society, the Long Branch Free Public Library, the Atlantic City Free Public Library, the Red Bank Public Library and the Monmouth County Library, including the Colts Neck Library's cookbook collection.

Thank you to Dr. Thomas Whitlow of Cornell University and Dr. Richard Veit of Monmouth University. Sincere thanks to Joal Leone, Jo Ann Vincent, Judy and Larry Wietsma, Liz Silva, Mark Stewart, Art Scott and to all those who shared thoughts or information about shore foods and eateries.

I'd like to extend a special thank-you to Whitney Tarella of The History Press. I'm grateful to my husband, Leon, for his love and technical support at the most difficult times, and I'm always thankful for my family: Greg (Max), Doug, Radha, Isa and Kieran...LYADYEFI!

Introduction

A land of magic, a land of wistfulness, a land of excitement, a land of mood. This is a land where today erases yesterday and prepares for tomorrow. This is the Jersey Shore.
—John T. Cunningham (1915–2012), This Is New Jersey, *1954*

There is great diversity in the foods and eateries of the Jersey Shore. The culinary history you are about to experience runs the gamut from elegant sit-down meals at Victorian hotels to hot dogs and ice cream at boardwalk stands. The varied gastronomy of the New Jersey coast includes mouthwatering pork roll sandwiches and thin-crust pizza, as well as farm-fresh veggies and luscious berries.

The story of food preparation along the New Jersey coast can be traced back to the Native Americans who were the region's original inhabitants. Roughly two thousand years ago, at the end of what archaeologists term the Archaic Period, and later during the Woodland Period, stone bowls and pottery vessels made it easier to prepare foods over an open fire. Much later, the story continues with the open-hearth cooking of early settlers and colonial tavern fare. However, this book begins in the mid-nineteenth century, when hotels were opening and tourism was blossoming along the Jersey coast. Boardwalks and food concessions soon followed. We can see how menus and eating habits changed as transportation improved with the coming of the railroads and then the automobile. *Jersey Shore Food History* explores iconic foods and famous eateries that have endured from the mid-nineteenth century through the mid-twentieth century and those that have been forgotten.

The geographic area included extends from Sandy Hook to Cape May and east of the Garden State Parkway. A few foods described are a bit farther inland. Many of the eateries featured are long gone. But some have been in operation since before the mid-twentieth century. A number of them have been owned by the same families for generations.

Although the book winds down with the post–World War II period, major chain restaurants and franchises from that era are not included. The only ones detailed are those that originated in the region as small individual stores. A chapter is devoted to farm products associated with the shore region. However, food businesses such as bakeries, dairies, grocery stores and bottlers are only mentioned. There was simply not enough space to include details about them in this work.

A smattering of vintage recipes is included for those readers who like to cook or simply enjoy reading them. The sources of the recipes are noted. Some are in their original form, but many of them have been adapted for modern times. The author does not take any responsibility for their success or failure.

Readers are encouraged to try the historic restaurants described that are still in operation and other Jersey Shore eateries not mentioned. There are a plethora of them! Many excellent books and guidebooks reviewing such places to eat are available in your local bookstore, online or at your public library. This work focuses on the past and simply whets the appetite for what is available today.

As a writer and historian, I've enjoyed delving into a variety of topics about the Jersey Shore, where I've lived for most of my life. I felt enthused about wanting to research and write about our food history. It's something that most people are interested in, at least some aspect of it. Everyone eats, most people cook and they dine, at least occasionally, at restaurants. I've never worked in or owned a restaurant or food business. I'm a self-taught cook and find that cooking can be fun, especially with my grandkids. I enjoy reading about food, watching TV cooking and travel shows and, most of all, eating!

Memories of going to dozens of New Jersey coast eateries while I was a kid in the 1950s and 1960s flood my mind. I can recall choosing a lobster at Hackney's in Atlantic City with my grandparents, who summered in Margate. And I enjoyed buying salt water taffy on the Atlantic City Boardwalk. Also, during that era, my parents traveled to Europe and took me along. In France, I quickly learned how to order *meules meuniére, steak au poivre* and a "Napoleon" for dessert. It was fabulous, but I always liked coming home to a sub sandwich and a frozen custard "down the shore."

While my sons were growing up, they enjoyed cooking, and they are great cooks as adults. We used to rotate kitchen duties, and family members could choose a recipe to prepare. As they grew, they gained valuable life experience working part time at shore area restaurants. In recent years, my husband (a terrific cook who bakes his own bread) and I have enjoyed traveling. We love the cuisine in Italy, but we have a special fondness for the Italian-American specialties and pizza at our Jersey Shore. We appreciate our local restaurants, where we can get almost any type of food within a small area. We've been blessed to live near such great establishments for eating out and to be able to cook at home with fresh seafood, veggies and fruits from the Garden State.

Like most people, I've become increasingly concerned about healthy eating and the quality of food we consume. But my goal for this book was to give an overview of food history at the Jersey Shore without making judgments. I've illustrated how local food and eateries developed from the mid-nineteenth century to the mid-twentieth century and how food has provided entertainment and boosted tourism.

"Foodie" is not a word I use to describe myself. I am simply a New Jersey writer who wants to share my passion for the history of our regional foods and eateries. Whether your interest lies in fresh seafood and produce, gourmet meals, casual dining or snacks at the beach, you'll find something delicious in these pages.

Victorian and Edwardian Delights

Rustic Vacations at First

As resort communities along the Jersey coast developed and grew during the mid-nineteenth century, the food offered on hotel menus became more elaborate. Eating evolved into an important feature of the seashore vacation. Visitors came for the clean air, sandy beaches and ocean bathing, and they also came to fill their bellies with gastronomic delights.

In the years following the American Revolution, simple boardinghouses dotted the Jersey coast. Well-to-do Philadelphians journeyed by horse-drawn vehicles over rough dirt roads to enjoy a respite from the heat. "Jersey wagons" or "oyster wagons" transported seafood from shore points to Trenton and Philadelphia. When they had room, they'd take passengers. Summer sojourners also came from New York and points north.

Taverns and inns were necessities in colonial times, not merely places for pleasure. Weary travelers stopped at these licensed establishments for needed nourishment and rest. One such place that exists today is the Smithville Inn on New York Road (Route 9, Galloway), once a well-traveled stagecoach route. When James Baremore built the inn in 1787, it was apparently intended to be his home. But he began taking in travelers and established a hospitality business that kept growing throughout the nineteenth century. Soon after 1900, the inn was abandoned. Then, in 1952, it was restored and reopened. Today, the Historic Smithville &

Village Greene, a tourist attraction with numerous shops and eateries, is adjacent to the popular inn.

There were no luxuries at the clapboard seaside boardinghouses in the early 1800s, but at least the rates were low. On Long Beach Island, the hosts fed their guests chicken, fish and oysters. The chicken and fish were served at the table, but the boarders were sent out to a pile under the shed for the oysters. There they could feel free to eat as many as they wanted to open![1] The meals at these rustic boardinghouses were mundane, but with the coming of big hotels, dining habits changed. The food became more varied and exciting.

Traveling on a boat or train was far more comfortable than bouncing up and down on a wagon or stagecoach as is it lumbered along muddy roads. By the mid-nineteenth century, a trip to the Jersey coast was no longer a grueling adventure; it had become a pleasant journey by sea or by rail. The ride provided a time to relax and enjoy a well-appointed meal.

The idea that eating less and choosing healthy foods would result in a longer, happier life had no place in the minds of most well-to-do Victorians. They appeared to believe in overindulgence as an accepted part of their lifestyle. Bigger was better. The more you ate, the more robust you would be…or so they thought. America was growing and expanding westward, and timesaving inventions were making life more enjoyable. Eating enormous meals represented the good life to those who could afford them.

However, the Victorian era also represents a time of great contrasts between rich and poor. While the resort hotel guests devoured big meals, workers in urban and industrial areas were struggling to feed their families. Pestilence, unsanitary conditions and hunger beleaguered much of the nation, and yet the small percentage of wealthy people indulged in luxuries.

A FOREIGN TOURIST'S VIEW

In 1850, Swedish novelist and feminist Fredrika Bremer wrote about her visit to Cape May. As far back as 1766, the *Philadelphia Gazette* stated that Cape May was a healthy place for sea bathing. Visitors flocked to the seaside town from Philadelphia, New York and other American cities. And tourists from Europe included the New Jersey coast in their itineraries. Cape May became known as "America's first resort."

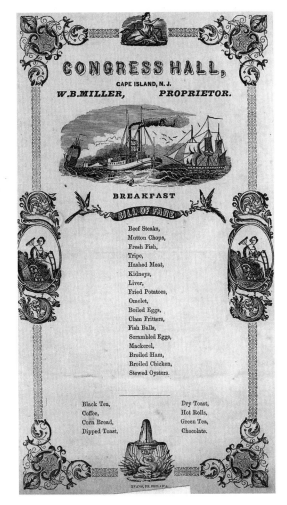

Above: A mid-nineteenth-century illustration of Cape May. *Courtesy of Congress Hall.*

Left: A breakfast menu from Congress Hall in Cape May, circa 1850. *Courtesy of Congress Hall.*

The forty-nine-year-old Fredrika had been touring North America for about a year and a half, keeping a journal of her observations. She traveled to Cape May by steamboat from Philadelphia with Professor Hart and his wife "on a beautiful July day." Her lively descriptions of the locally grown veggies and details about the wait staff at the Columbia House are best told in her own words:

> *There sit, in a large light hall, at two tables about three hundred persons, while a thundering band is playing, waited upon by a regiment of somewhat above forty negroes, who march in and maneuver to the sound of a bell, and make as much noise as they possibly can make with dishes and plates, and such like things, and that is not a little. They come marching in two and two, each one carrying a dish or bowl in his hands…*
>
> *The dinners are for the most part, very good, and the dishes less highly seasoned than I have been accustomed to find them at American tables, and especially at the hotels. Although I here always find a deficiency of vegetables yet I am fond of one which is called "squash" and which is the flesh of a species of very common gourd here, boiled and served up much in the style of our cabbage, and which is eaten with meat. It is white, somewhat insipid, but soft and agreeable, rather like spinach; it is here universally eaten; so also are tomatoes, a very savory and delicately acid fruit, which is eaten as salad. On the second course I dare not venture to eat anything but sago pudding or custard, a kind of egg-cream in cups, and am glad that these are always to be had here.*

Fredrika penned her observations about Jersey corn. She provided insight as to how some of the clientele in the Cape May hotel dining hall were quite voracious:

> *One standing dish at American tables at this season is the so-called "sweet corn." It is the entire corn ear of a peculiar kind of maize, which ripens early. It is boiled in water and served whole; it is eaten with butter and tastes like French "petit pois" (little peas) they scrape off the grains with a knife or cut them out from the stem. Some people take the whole stem and gnaw them out with their teeth; two gentlemen do so who sit opposite Professor Hart and myself at table, and whom we call "the sharks" because of their remarkable ability in gobbling up large and often double portions of everything which comes to table, and it really troubles me to see how their wide mouths, furnished with able teeth, ravenously grind up the beautiful white, pearly maize ears, which I saw so lately in their wedding attire, and which are now massacred, and disappear down the ravenous throats of the sharks.[2]*

THE RISE OF "THE BRANCH"

At Long Branch, the first boardinghouse opened in about 1788. Larger "houses," or hotels, were soon built. The resort mushroomed and became a popular destination for New Yorkers and Philadelphians escaping oppressive city heat.

In 1865, the railroad line that ran from New York to Eatontown was extended four miles to coastal Long Branch. This created a boom in tourism and land sales. Situated on a natural bluff, Long Branch proved to be an ideal location for entrepreneurs to build hotels.

When President Ulysses S. Grant made an Elberon cottage his family's summer home in 1869, the popularity of the Long Branch area increased dramatically. Grant attended dinners and dances at the big hotels but was said to eat simple meals. He did enjoy the typical big Victorian breakfast, and he had a well-known passion for rice pudding.

By the 1870s, Long Branch was dubbed the "American Brighton" after the famed British watering place. It rivaled the prestigious American resorts of Saratoga Springs in New York and Newport, Rhode Island. The Monmouth Park Race Track, opened in 1870, and the stylish gambling houses provided

The Mansion House at Long Branch was typical of the Victorian oceanfront hotels. First Lady Mary Lincoln stayed here in 1861. Even while the Civil War was raging, well-to-do vacationers were occupied with carefree summer activities. A plaque commemorating the Mansion House and Mrs. Lincoln's visit was installed at its former location by the Long Branch Historical Association in 2011. The site is now Pier Village, a modern complex with shops and restaurants. *From* Frank Leslie's Illustrated Newspaper, *August 1, 1863.*

An illustration of the Mansion House dining hall gives an idea of how hectic the meal times were at the Long Branch grand hotels. A supervisor is seen directing the waiters. *From* Frank Leslie's Illustrated Newspaper, *July 15 1865.*

major attractions for vacationers. Though still a popular destination, Cape May became somewhat less frequented after the Civil War. Many of the resort's prominent visitors were southern plantation owners who could no longer afford high-end seaside vacations during the era of Reconstruction.

SPARTAN DINING HALLS

The dining rooms at the oceanfront hotels were surprisingly austere, with none of the plush décor found in the lobbies and parlors. Victorian furnishings meant velvet sofas with puffy seats, jardinières, bucolic paintings in gilt frames, oriental rugs and heavy damask drapes. But the enormous dining rooms looked like military mess halls, with neat rows of rectangular tables and utilitarian chairs. They did have plain white tablecloths, and vases of flowers were sometimes placed on tables.

Apparently, there was a good reason for the unadorned look of the dining halls—cleanliness. The areas with food had to be kept spotless for fear of rodents, bugs or simply dust that could build up. Sanitary conditions were becoming a big concern.

On the other hand, the food and clothing were far from spartan. French fashions, and indeed everything French, was admired and imitated at

The hustle and bustle in the dining hall at Leland's Ocean Hotel, Long Branch. *From* Frank Leslie's Illustrated Newspaper, *July 6, 1872.*

American resorts. Gastronomy based on French cooking methods was all the rage in Victorian America. The menu selections were often in French and sometimes anglicized, or the English translation of a dish would appear in parentheses, or vice versa.

The hotel menus did not list prices (except for alcoholic drinks), indicating that meals were included with the cost of the rooms. Though the dining rooms were plain, the meals were elaborately presented. Some of the specialized serving dishes and utensils are with us today; others are seen only in museums or antique shops.

RECIPES FOR AN 1873 HOTEL DINNER

Three recipes are provided here for selections offered on the 1873 West End Hotel (Long Branch) menu. They have been somewhat updated so they can be used by the modern cook.

Mock Turtle Soup

Green turtle soup was so popular that no meal seemed complete without it. If the catch of the day did not include a large sea turtle, the chef had to improvise with ingredients at hand, and so we have *mock* turtle soup.

VEAL STOCK
3 pounds veal breast
4 ounces ham
2 carrots, coarsely chopped
2 celery ribs, coarsely chopped
1 onion, chopped
1 bay leaf
4 cloves
4 sprigs parsley
½ teaspoon thyme
1 tablespoon salt
about 12 cups water

Place all the ingredients, including about 12 cups of water, in a large kettle (stock pot). Bring to a boil and simmer about 4 hours. Remove the meat and strain the broth. Chill thoroughly and remove the cake of fat that forms on the top. Remove the meat from the bones and dice. Set aside.

VEAL BALLS
¾ pound chopped veal
1 tablespoon parsley
1 teaspoon lemon peel
1 egg

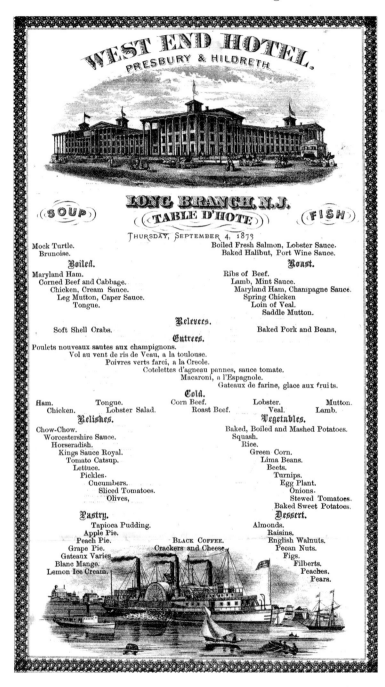

WEST END HOTEL.
PRESBURY & HILDRETH.

LONG BRANCH, N.J.
TABLE D'HOTE

((SOUP))   (FISH)

THURSDAY, SEPTEMBER 4, 1873

Mock Turtle.
Brunoise.

Boiled Fresh Salmon, Lobster Sauce.
Baked Halibut, Port Wine Sauce.

Boiled.
Maryland Ham.
Corned Beef and Cabbage.
Chicken, Cream Sauce.
Leg Mutton, Caper Sauce.
Tongue.

Roast.
Ribs of Beef.
Lamb, Mint Sauce.
Maryland Ham, Champagne Sauce.
Spring Chicken.
Loin of Veal.
Saddle Mutton.

Relevees.
Soft Shell Crabs.

Baked Pork and Beans,

Entrees.
Poulets nouveaux sautes aux champignons.
Vol au vent de ris de Veau, a la toulouse.
Poivres verts farci, a la Creole.
Cotelettes d'agneau pannes, sauce tomate.
Macaroni, a l'Espagnole.
Gateaux de farine, glace aux fruits.

Cold.
Ham.   Tongue.   Corn Beef.   Lobster.   Mutton.
Chicken.   Lobster Salad.   Roast Beef.   Veal.   Lamb.

Relishes.
Chow-Chow.
Worcestershire Sauce.
Horseradish.
Kings Sauce Royal.
Tomato Catsup.
Lettuce.
Pickles.
Cucumbers.
Sliced Tomatoes.
Olives,

Vegetables.
Baked, Boiled and Mashed Potatoes.
Squash.
Rice.
Green Corn.
Lima Beans.
Beets.
Turnips.
Egg Plant.
Onions.
Stewed Tomatoes.
Baked Sweet Potatoes.

Pastry.
Tapioca Pudding.
Apple Pie.
Peach Pie.
Grape Pie.
Gateaux Varies.
Blanc Mange.
Lemon Ice Cream.

BLACK COFFEE.
Crackers and Cheese.

Dessert.
Almonds.
Raisins.
English Walnuts.
Pecan Nuts.
Figs.
Filberts.
Peaches.
Pears.

An 1873 dinner menu from the West End Hotel at Long Branch. Notice that the "relevee," a dish that we'd think of as a main course today, was often consumed after the appetizer and before the main course. *Courtesy of Special Collections and University Archives, Rutgers University Libraries.*

1 tablespoon flour
1 teaspoon salt
¼ teaspoon black pepper
6 tablespoons butter

Combine all the ingredients except the butter. Roll into small balls and sauté in the butter until browned.

ASSEMBLING THE SOUP
6 tablespoons flour
butter from the veal balls
1 cup cooled stock
remaining strained stock
1 cup medium sherry
1 teaspoon salt
½ teaspoon cayenne pepper
1 teaspoon Worcestershire sauce

Garnish: 2 eggs, hard-cooked, sliced; 1 lemon, sliced

In a large kettle, stir the flour into the melted butter. Blend in the cooled stock and cook until it is thickened. Gradually add the remaining stock. Bring this to a boil, stirring to blend. Add the sherry, salt, cayenne, pepper and Worcestershire sauce. Add the veal pieces and veal balls. Serve in heated bowls. Garnish with sliced egg and lemon.[3] Serves 6.

Breaded Lamb Cutlets with Tomato Sauce

To give a formal, cosmopolitan flavor to its menu, the West End Hotel in Long Branch listed this dish as *Cotelettes d'agneau pannes with sauce tomate*. For a less sophisticated dinner, it listed corned beef and baked pork and beans on the same menu.
4 to 8 lamb cutlets (depending on size)
salt and black pepper (to taste)
2 to 3 egg yolks, beaten
2 cups breadcrumbs
shortening

Pound each cutlet to about ½ to ¾ of an inch thick. Sprinkle lightly with salt and black pepper. Dip each cutlet into the beaten egg yolks and then into the breadcrumbs, coating well. Melt the shortening in a heavy frying pan. Sauté the cutlets over low heat, turning often, until they are brown and cooked through. Serve warm with tomato sauce.

TOMATO SAUCE
1 cup stewed tomatoes (fresh or canned)
1 onion slice
1 cup beef broth
2 teaspoons sugar
½ teaspoon salt (or salt to taste)
¼ teaspoon black pepper
4 tablespoons butter
4 tablespoons flour
1 tablespoon vinegar

In a blender, blend the tomatoes and onion slice. (For a seedless sauce, sieve the tomato before blending it with the onion.) Pour into a saucepan and mix in the beef broth, sugar, salt and black pepper. Heat to a slow boil.

In a saucepan, melt the butter over low heat, browning it lightly. Stir in the flour with a wooden spoon and cook, stirring constantly, until the mixture is smooth and starting to bubble. Pour in the tomato-beef broth mixture slowly, stirring vigorously. Boil slowly for 1 minute. Reduce the heat to a simmer. Add the vinegar and stir well. Continue to simmer for 10 minutes, stirring often. Pour the sauce over the lamb cutlets and serve at once. Yields 2 cups. Serves 4.

Blancmange

French for "white food," blancmange developed in the Middle Ages but not as a dessert. By the seventeenth century, however, it had become a gelatin dessert made with sweetened white wine and ground almonds. Some Victorian cookbooks continued to favor the older gelatin type, but most preferred to use the more fashionable cornstarch method of making blancmange.

¼ cup sugar
4 tablespoons cornstarch
⅛ teaspoon salt
2 cups milk
½ teaspoon almond flavoring (optional)
1 cup strawberries or raspberries, crushed and sweetened to taste (or 4 tablespoons strawberry or raspberry preserves.

In the top half of a double boiler, combine the sugar, cornstarch and salt. Mix with ½ cup of the milk to make a smooth paste. In a saucepan, bring the remaining milk to a slow boil, stirring constantly. Gradually stir the boiling milk into the cornstarch mixture. Mix well. Cook the blancmange over boiling water, stirring constantly, until smooth and thickened. Cover the top of the double boiler and cook for 10 minutes longer, stirring every 2 minutes. Remove from the heat and add the almond flavoring, if desired.

Rinse four ½-cup molds or custard cups with cold water. Pour in the blancmange and chill. Unmold onto serving plates and serve with the crushed berries or berry preserves. Serves 4.

Descriptions and recipes for mock turtle soup, breaded lamb cutlets with tomato sauce and blancmange are from The Victorian Seaside Cookbook. *Courtesy of the New Jersey Historical Society.*

CELEBRITY CHEFS

Well-respected chefs from the big cities were hired for the shore Victorian hotels. They were no doubt as anxious to get away from the heat of the city for the summer as the vacationers were. "Celebrity chefs," as they are called today, are not a completely new phenomenon. We simply have more media to promote them than the Victorians did, as well as more people entering the profession. Chefs of yesteryear probably would have loved to be on television cooking shows if only such technology had existed.

Even though they didn't watch chefs cooking, the Victorians idolized famous French chefs, especially Auguste Escoffier (1846–1935). In 1894, French-born American chef Charles Ranhofer first published an enormous volume of gastronomy, *The Epicurean*. Ranhofer was head chef at New York's renowned Delmonico's.

Little is known about nineteenth-century hotel and restaurant kitchens, but some descriptions can be found in the newspapers and brochures of the day. In 1874, M. Jules Harder, the head chef employed by the huge Leland's Ocean Hotel at Long Branch reportedly had a staff of eight male cooks and ten female assistants. Harder's kitchen included ten furnaces and three broiler fires—one for fish, another for beef steaks and the third for mutton chops. A brick oven provided the ideal conditions for baking potatoes, and two big copper cauldrons served as stock boilers. The line of cooking ranges was seventy-five feet long. A "bain-marie" that contained a hot water bath kept the many sauces warm.

POTATOES LONG BRANCH

In *The Epicurean* by Charles Ranhofer, recipe #2792 is for "Potatoes Long Branch (Pommes de Terre Long Branch)." Each potato was pared into one continuous curl that could be as long as a yard or two. This was accomplished with a special gadget that is illustrated in Ranhofer's book but which could be done by hand. The long curls were soaked in cold water for about two hours, deep fried in fat until crispy and golden brown, drained and salted.[4] This novelty, also called curled potatoes, was a big hit with Victorian vacationers. Perhaps they could be considered the ancestor of today's curly fries, although they were served at sit-down dinners rather than as a casual snack.

Saratoga Chips, which might be compared to today's potato chips, originated at the well-established resort of Saratoga Springs in New York State, a competitor of Long Branch. These potatoes showed up on menus at the finest hotels and restaurants. Potatoes Long Branch may have been developed to surpass them in popularity, but it was the Saratoga style that endured.

This page and opposite: This 1870s wine list, with an irresistible "Naughty Boy" on its cover, is from Leland's Ocean Hotel at Long Branch. *Courtesy of Special Collections and University Archives, Rutgers University Libraries.*

OCEAN HOTEL WINES.

Champagnes.

	PTS.	QTS.
Veuve Clicquot, Yellow Label	$1.75	$3.50
Pommery Sec	1.75	3.50
G. H. Mumm's Extra Dry	1.75	3.50
Piper Heidsieck	1.50	3.00
Dry Monopole	1.75	3.50
Delmonico	1.75	3.50
L. Roderer's Carte Blanche	1.75	3.50

Clarets.

CUZOL FILS & CO.

	PTS.	QTS.
Vin Ordinaire	30	50
Medoc	40	60
Floirac	50	80
St. Estephe	70	1.25
St. Julien, Superior	80	1.50
Pontet Canet	1.00	2.00
Chateau La Rose	1.25	2.50
Chateau Lafite, 1874	1.75	3.50
Chateau Margaux, 1874	2.00	4.00

Sauternes.

Barsac	50	85
Sauterne	75	1.50
Haut Sauternes	80	1.50
Latour Blanche	1.00	2.00
Chateau Y-quem, 1874	2.00	4.00

Burgundy.

Macon	70	1.25
Nuits	1.00	2.00
Chambertin	1.50	3.00
" 1865, quarts only	..	3.50
Clos de Vougeot	..	4.00
Chablis (white)	75	1.50
Hermitage (white)	..	3.50

Rhine Wines.

Laubenheimer	40	75
Hochheimer	60	1.00
Geisenheimer	70	1.25
Deidesheimer	80	1.50
Rudesheimer	1.00	2.00
Steinberger, Cabinet	..	3.00
Johannisberger (Schloss)	..	4.00

Sherry.

Table	80	1.50
Topaz	1.00	2.00
Cabinet	1.25	2.50
Montilla	1.50	3.00
Amontillado	2.00	4.00
Old Solera	2.50	5.00

Madeira.

Old East India	2.50	5.00
Victoria Royal	1.50	3.00
Ivanhoe	2.00	4.00

Port.

	PTS.	QTS.
Old Port	$1.00	$2.00
London Dock	1.25	2.50
White Port	2.00	4.00
Sandeman, Pure Juice	1.50	3.00

Whiskies, Brandies, Etc.

Monogram Club Rye	2.00
Kentucky Valley, Nelson Co., Bourbon	2.00
Private Stock Cabinet	3.00
Hennessey S. O. P.	3.00
" V. S. O. P.	5.00
" 1848	7.00
Blackberry Brandy	2.00
Monmouth Apple Jack	2.00
Holland Gin	2.00
Old Tom Gin	2.00
St. Croix, Royal Crown	2.50
Jamaica Rum, London Club	3.00

Cordials and Liqueurs.

Vermouth per glass	20
Chartreuse	20
Curacoa	20
Maraschino or Anisette	20
Kirschwasser	20
Absinthe	20
Benedictine	20
Kummel	20

Ales, Porters, Etc.

New York Lager Beer	15
Milwaukee Lager	20
" Export Beer	25
Bohemian Beer, P. B.	30
Clausen's Champagne Lager	20
Imported Tivoli Beer	30
" Kaiser Beer	30
" Culmbach	30
Bass' Ale, India Pale, Dauke's	30
" White Label	30
Muir's Scotch Ale	30
Guinness' Stout	30
Ginger Ale, C. & C., Belfast	25
Cider (extra), pint, 30c.; quart	60

Mineral Waters, Etc.

Apollinaris	25	40
Clysmic	..	40
Congress	25	..
Hathorn	25	..
German Seltzer, per jug	..	35
Syphon Seltzer, C. S.	..	25
Syphon Vichy, "	..	25
Hunyadi Water	40	..

What to Drink?

Vintage hotel menus tell us that the selection of wines was ordered by pints or quarts (this referred to the bottles). Champagne, Madeira and port were favorites in Victorian times. But obviously a wide variety of spirits was available, mostly imported. Local "Monmouth Applejack"[5] is listed in the hard liquor section. Applejack was commonly known as "Jersey Lightning," giving a clue to its potency.

Another popular drink (not on the menu illustrated) was a Jersey Cocktail Iced: "For three cocktails, put into a vermuth [sic] glass some applejack and two glassfuls of Italian or French vermuth, adding three dashes of Angostura bitters and finely pounded ice. Cover with a tin shaker, toss, strain and pour into small glasses."[6]

Mineral waters, including the Congress brand from Saratoga Springs and Apollinaris (sparkling German water), were well liked with meals and considered to be cure-alls. Vendors sold Saratoga brand water on the Atlantic City Boardwalk in the late nineteenth-century alongside root beer and sarsaparilla.

Come to the Jersey Shore!

New hotels cropped up all along the Jersey coast as increasing numbers of vacationers scrambled for accommodations. The completion of a railroad line from Camden to Absecon in 1854 got the ball rolling, and it kept increasing in speed. Railroads promoted the Jersey resorts with advertisements and brochures. Cape May remained a well-liked resort, but Long Branch and then Atlantic City grew to be the major destinations with high style, amusements, drinking and gambling. The quieter Methodist towns such as Ocean Grove were also luring visitors, but with camp meetings and tent communities that brought many pious visitors. Remote areas such as Long Beach Island attracted fishermen and duck hunters who stayed in shanties and cabins. However, there were some elegant accommodations at hotels such as the Engleside at Beach Haven. Sea Bright, Asbury Park, Belmar (known as Ocean Beach at first), Spring Lake, Bay Head, Point Pleasant Beach and scores of other coastal

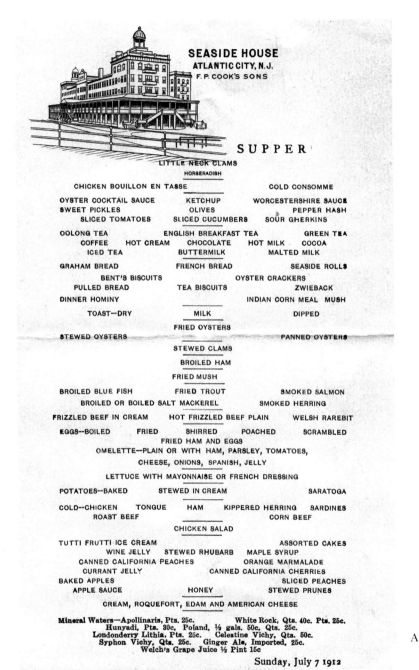

SEASIDE HOUSE
ATLANTIC CITY, N.J.
F. P. COOK'S SONS

SUPPER

LITTLE NECK CLAMS
HORSERADISH

CHICKEN BOUILLON EN TASSE		COLD CONSOMME

OYSTER COCKTAIL SAUCE	KETCHUP	WORCESTERSHIRE SAUCE
SWEET PICKLES	OLIVES	PEPPER HASH
SLICED TOMATOES	SLICED CUCUMBERS	SOUR GHERKINS

OOLONG TEA	ENGLISH BREAKFAST TEA	GREEN TEA
COFFEE HOT CREAM	CHOCOLATE HOT MILK	COCOA
ICED TEA	BUTTERMILK	MALTED MILK

GRAHAM BREAD	FRENCH BREAD	SEASIDE ROLLS
BENT'S BISCUITS	OYSTER CRACKERS	
PULLED BREAD	TEA BISCUITS	ZWIEBACK
DINNER HOMINY		INDIAN CORN MEAL MUSH

TOAST--DRY	MILK	DIPPED

FRIED OYSTERS

STEWED OYSTERS		PANNED OYSTERS

STEWED CLAMS

BROILED HAM

FRIED MUSH

BROILED BLUE FISH	FRIED TROUT	SMOKED SALMON
BROILED OR BOILED SALT MACKEREL		SMOKED HERRING

FRIZZLED BEEF IN CREAM	HOT FRIZZLED BEEF PLAIN	WELSH RAREBIT

EGGS--BOILED	FRIED	SHIRRED	POACHED	SCRAMBLED

FRIED HAM AND EGGS

OMELETTE--PLAIN OR WITH HAM, PARSLEY, TOMATOES,
CHEESE, ONIONS, SPANISH, JELLY

LETTUCE WITH MAYONNAISE OR FRENCH DRESSING

POTATOES--BAKED	STEWED IN CREAM	SARATOGA

COLD--CHICKEN TONGUE	HAM	KIPPERED HERRING	SARDINES
ROAST BEEF		CORN BEEF	

CHICKEN SALAD

TUTTI FRUTTI ICE CREAM		ASSORTED CAKES
WINE JELLY STEWED RHUBARB	MAPLE SYRUP	
CANNED CALIFORNIA PEACHES	ORANGE MARMALADE	
CURRANT JELLY	CANNED CALIFORNIA CHERRIES	
BAKED APPLES		SLICED PEACHES
APPLE SAUCE	HONEY	STEWED PRUNES

CREAM, ROQUEFORT, EDAM AND AMERICAN CHEESE

Mineral Waters—Apollinaris, Pts. 25c.   White Rock, Qts. 40c. Pts. 25c.
Hunyadi, Pts. 30c, Poland, ½ gals. 50c, Qts. 25c.
Londonderry Lithia, Pts. 25c.   Celestine Vichy, Qts. 50c.
Syphon Vichy, Qts. 25c.   Ginger Ale, Imported, 25c.
Welch's Grape Juice ½ Pint 15c

A

Sunday, July 7 1912

1912 supper menu for the Seaside House on the Atlantic City Boardwalk included cornmeal mush. (Dinner was held at about noon, and supper was a lighter meal served at about 6:00 p.m.). *Courtesy of Special Collections and University Archives, Rutgers University Libraries.*

33

towns also proved to be profitable places for Victorian entrepreneurs to invest in hotels.

It didn't take long for the culinary delights of other resorts to become as well known as those of Long Branch. Atlantic City's Brighton Hotel (a Victorian hotel on the Boardwalk torn down in 1959) was famous for its illustrious "Brighton Punch." The recipe for the beverage was a well-kept secret, although "experts insisted it had a rye base well-seasoned with strong black Jamaica rum." Many tales are told about its origin, including one that a bartender discovered it quite by accident on a rainy day.[7] A former bellhop at the hotel swore that no one ever revealed the exact recipe, but a close approximation is as follows: 1½ ounce rye (100 proof), 1 ounce dark rum, 1 teaspoon brown sugar and the juice of half a lemon; shake with cracked ice fifteen times, pour into a tall glass and add a half slice of orange.[8]

AN ERA OF CONSPICUOUS CONSUMPTION

The upper classes had more leisure time than ever, as well as money to spend. This was evident in the restaurants and hotels of the Gilded Age. In his 1991 book, *America Eats Out: An Illustrated History of Restaurants, Taverns, Coffee Shops, Speakeasies, and Other Establishments That Have Fed Us for 350 Years,* John Mariani titled the chapter about the Victorian/Edwardian era "The Age of Gluttony." Overeating was not just accepted; it was condoned.

During this era of conspicuous consumption, the hotels at the Jersey coast resorts satisfied their guests' appetites with vast quantities of food. According to author and historian George H. Moss Jr.:

> *Daily food consumption at the height of the season at the Ocean Hotel in Long Branch included 900 pounds of fish, 1,500 pounds of meat, four barrels of potatoes as well as chickens by the hundreds and vegetables by the dozen basketfuls. The chief baker and confectioner had six assistants to help them make the ice cream, pies, pastry cakes and bread. They used three barrels of flour and 400 eggs a day—and don't forget milk, butter, sugar and all the other ingredients that produced a fine cuisine.*

THE BIGGEST EATER?

Most wealthy Victorians didn't seem to give much thought to portion control. They ate many, though certainly not all, of the courses offered on the menus. Women wanted an hourglass figure and sucked their waists in with tight-fitting corsets, though some feisty women did experiment with diets and exercise.

Stories about the eating habits of one historical figure of the time are legendary. James Buchanan Brady, better known as "Diamond Jim" was a self-made millionaire. Brady worked his way up from bellboy to railroad supply tycoon. He is most often remembered for his flashy jewelry and flamboyant dining. His physique was described as "corpulent."

Brady frequented New York "lobster palaces," as well as restaurants at the New Jersey Shore and Saratoga Springs. He was often accompanied by the glamorous and buxom entertainer Lillian Russell, who was also reputed to be a big eater. Stories are told describing how the two of them enjoyed having eating contests. Lillian and Diamond Jim visited Long Branch, attended the horse races at Monmouth Race Track and caused a sensation by riding down Ocean Avenue in Brady's electric automobile. The pair was also said to be somewhat weight conscious when they began exercising by riding bejeweled bicycles that Diamond Jim had custom made.

Diamond Jim, a biography by Parker Morell, was published in 1934, seventeen years after Brady's death. In his colorful interpretation of Brady's life, Morell described the millionaire's huge appetite:

> *Jim started things off in the morning with a light breakfast of beefsteak, a few chops, eggs, flapjacks, fried potatoes, hominy, corn-bread, a few muffins, and a huge beaker of milk. He never touched tea or coffee. Brady's drink of choice was orange juice and he never drank any alcohol. After breakfast, he'd have a snack of oysters and clams followed by lunch which generally consisted of more oysters and clams, a devilled crab or two or three, perhaps a pair of broiled lobsters, then a joint of beef or another steak, a salad, and several kinds of fruit pie. Jim also liked to finish off this meal with the better part of a box of chocolate candies. It made the food set better, he figured.*

Although he was indeed a big eater and overweight, it's likely that his actual consumption has been exaggerated. An article by David Kamp in the

December 30, 2008 *New York Times* gives reasons why Brady's eating capacity couldn't possibly have been as large as reported. But even if the stories of his huge meals were tall tales, Brady certainly personified the era of gluttony.

Diamond Jim was weakened by medical conditions that were likely aggravated by his overeating. Brady maintained a suite of rooms at the Shelburne Hotel in Atlantic City where, on April 13, 1917, he died in his sleep at the age of sixty-one.

ALFRESCO DINING

At times, the Victorians abandoned the formalities of their regular meals and ventured outdoors to eat. Although fast-food restaurants as we know them today did not yet exist, excursions to the countryside surrounding the coastal resorts included casual outdoor dining. Humid weather, mosquitoes and ants presented challenges but did not deter the vacationers from enjoying these outings.

Actress and women's rights advocate Olive Logan was a prolific author who wrote about Long Branch in an 1876 *Harper's Monthly* article. In her flowery style, she described her stay at the resort city, including side trips to the surrounding rural areas:

> *The morning being usually devoted to the bath, the afternoon is set apart for excursions and drives. At a special festivity at Pleasure Bay such as a clam-bake or a regatta, you are liable to meet the most important people at the Branch. The President himself has at times deigned to attend a clam-bake. Pleasure Bay is a charming drive from the centre of gayety at the Branch, just a mile and a half through a lovely open country to an old-fashioned New Jersey tavern in the midst of a green grove on the bank of a placid sheet of water…A fairy-like yacht with spreading sail receives you at the water's edge, and you are blown over to the opposite shore, where, with a chunk of fish on the end of a string, and a net at the end of a pole, you find that catching crabs is as easy as eating them. The sail gives you a glorious appetite and if there is a clam-bake when you return, you will proceed to eat ravenously of a conglomeration of green corn, clams, crabs, potatoes, and yellow-legged chickens.*

Clambakes, often associated with New England, were also popular at the Jersey Shore. In 1907, waiters are ready to serve clams on the banks of the Shrewsbury River by Wardell's Port-Au-Peck restaurant (near Long Branch). *Pach photograph from* Those Innocent Years *by Moss and Schnitzspahn.*

STORM WARRIORS WERE GOOD COOKS

Similar to firefighters, who are well known as capable cooks, the men of the United States Life-Saving Service excelled in culinary arts. Along the Jersey coast in the late nineteenth and early twentieth centuries, the surfmen, fondly described by the media as "Storm Warriors," were known to prepare healthy and delicious foods. Most of their stations were quite isolated from stores and restaurants, so the men prepared their meals.

The Life-Saving Service formally began in 1848 with the Newell Act, named for its principal advocate, New Jersey representative William A. Newell. Congress appropriated funds to establish the agency as a response to the numerous shipwrecks along the treacherous coast. In 1915, it merged

Surfmen were reputed to be good cooks. These unidentified members of the United States Life-Saving Service were possibly stationed at Long Branch or Monmouth Beach.

with the United States Revenue Cutter Service to become the United States Coast Guard. In its heyday, there were forty-one Life-Saving stations on the New Jersey coast. Only a few of these structures remain. Recipes used by Jersey surfmen have not been found, but if they did write them down, perhaps they'll turn up someday.

Most stations had a crew of seven, including the head keeper, and as new men replaced retiring ones, they were expected to know how to cook. Because the rookies had already served as substitutes, they had some experience cooking for the crew. The men would rotate kitchen duty. Although some stations along the East Coast hired cooks, most of the Jersey surfmen reportedly did their own cooking. Survivors from shipwrecks were often brought to the stations, where they were clothed and fed.

In an interview for the *Asbury Park Journal* of January 12, 1900, a retired New Jersey surfman filled his pipe and chatted with a reporter:

> *I often read about these chefs who do the cooking for the millionaires and get enormous salaries. In my opinion they get more than they are really worth for there are so many Americans who could do the work as well. Today there*

is a small army of men doing service in Uncle Sam's life-saving stations along the coast who are the best of cooks.

The coastal heroes even baked their own bread, pies and cakes. The retired lifesaver praised their work: "And such bread! It is none of the chaff, dosed with alum and bad water that is handed out in many of the city bakeshops."

The wives and children of the men usually lived as close as possible to the isolated stations, and some even occupied small beach cottages nearby. The surfmen admitted that they learned to cook from wives, sweethearts, mothers and grandmothers. The women often pitched in when needed to help with duties, including cooking and caring for shipwreck survivors.

Dinner could be found right outside the station's door. A fishing pole, or a gun, was all they needed. Surfmen were known for preparing fish and wild fowl, which were plentiful in the marshy areas. Ducks, geese, snipe and other shorebirds that were popular items at the stations were also cooked by gourmet chefs and were served at fancy shore hotels and restaurants.

The retired surfman concluded the interview with this: "There are no better fed men in the country than the life-saving crews."

SHOREBIRD COOKERY

Cookery books from the nineteenth and early twentieth centuries include recipes for various game birds that were hunted along the Jersey coast. Although there are still some marshes and woods for hunting that have been preserved, much of the land in these coastal areas is now developed. Today, certain open areas are designated as sanctuaries for wildlife. At the Jersey Shore in the Victorian/Edwardian times, shorebirds were common fare on menus, but they are offered only occasionally today. Indeed, some of the birds eaten long ago are now endangered species.

Squab Bordelaise

Reed birds bordelaise was a popular Jersey Shore dish in the 1880s. But since the tiny reed bird is not available today, squab has been substituted.

6 1-pound squabs
3 tablespoons of butter
1 teaspoon each salt and paprika

Place the squabs on a broiler rack 4 inches from the flame. Combine the butter, salt and paprika. Brush the squabs generously with the butter. Broil 10 to 15 minutes or until tender. Do not overcook. The birds may also be roasted at 375° for 30 to 35 minutes. Serve with sauce bordelaise.

SAUCE BORDELAISE
3 tablespoons scallions, chopped
1 clove garlic, minced
2 tablespoons butter
1 cup each red wine and beef stock
2 tablespoons tomato paste
1 tablespoon cornstarch
salt and black pepper (to taste)
1 teaspoon lemon juice
1 teaspoon parsley, chopped

Sauté the scallions and garlic in the butter until softened. Add the wine and beef stock and boil to reduce to 1½ cups. Stir in the tomato paste. Dissolve the cornstarch in a small amount of water and add to the sauce, stirring constantly. Cook until slightly thickened. Add salt and black pepper to taste, and stir in the lemon juice and parsley. Yields 2 cups. Serves 6.

Description and Recipe from The Victorian Seaside Cookbook. *Courtesy of the New Jersey Historical Society.*

SHIFTING SANDS

By the close of the nineteenth century, the character of the shore region had changed. An increased flow of day-trippers came to the coastal resorts by steamboat, train and, ultimately, by automobile. People had more leisure time, and transportation had become faster and more affordable. These middle-class visitors did not have the money for an extended stay at a posh hotel. Instead, they enjoyed a day at the beach and looked for places where they could eat well but reasonably. Moderately priced restaurants began to crop up. In Atlantic City, Childs restaurants, established in 1889 by Samuel and William Childs, claimed to be the first to use a cafeteria-type style, with trays and self-service. Also in Atlantic City, Kents was a well-liked small chain founded as Kents Restaurant and Baking Company in 1903 by Morris Walton.

The picnic meal or box-type lunch became a popular way for the excursionist to eat. By the 1920s, day-trippers were called "shoobies," the most popular explanation being that they brought their food along in shoeboxes. At the same time, members of the wealthier classes began to take vacations at greater distances as transportation improved and more resorts sprang up in various distant parts of the country—such as Florida and the Rocky Mountains.

PRESERVATION AND TECHNOLOGY

Salt was once an important commodity along the Jersey coast. In the mid-1700s, salt works flourished at locations including the Shark River area, Long Beach Island and Little Egg Harbor, among others. Salt was important for preserving food as well as for gunpowder. Skirmishes occurred during the Revolutionary War as the British targeted salt works and set afire the ones near present-day Belmar. Eventually, the importance of salt processing plants diminished along the coast as salt was imported from other areas and became less necessary for food preservation.

Refrigerated railroad cars first went into use shortly after the Civil War and expanded the types of food available for home and restaurant use. With the industrial revolution came improvements in food production such as the "canning line," which increased the number of canned foods. Considered to be marvelous inventions of their day, packaged and processed foods rapidly became commonplace items in most households. Synthetic chemicals that could alter the growing and processing of food were beginning to be manufactured and used with increasing frequency.

Consumers craved more fresh beef and had less interest in cured meat products such as corned beef and salted pork that were popular in the colonial tavern days. But unsanitary conditions in the slaughtering and meatpacking industries were causing health problems. Interestingly, it was a novel that increased awareness and helped to improve the deplorable practices of the meat business. *The Jungle* (1906) by Upton Sinclair exposed conditions that led to the passage of the Wiley Act, more commonly known as the Pure Food and Drug Act of 1906.

A President's Shore Dinner

In the early twentieth century, there were only scattered restaurants outside the major Jersey Shore resort towns, as highway diners and fast-food places had not yet been established. However, there were roadhouses and quaint inns along the main routes. In Forked River, the Greyhound Inn on South Main Street was advertised as the "Best Over Night Stop between New York and Atlantic City." The surrounding area on Barnegat Bay was popular for fishing and gunning, and the inn's distinctive décor reflected these activities. Elaborate menus featured local specialties of venison and shorebird dishes.

On September 9, probably 1916, President Woodrow Wilson stayed at the Greyhound Inn on his way back from Atlantic City to his summer residence at Long Branch.[9] The president and his wife were heartily welcomed by the inn's proprietor.

The president and Mrs. Wilson and their party enjoyed "a real Shore and Chicken Dinner" and were said to remark that it was one of the best dinners they ever had. The couple thanked the owner, Mr. Briggs, and left for Shadow Lawn,[10] their residence at Long Branch, the summer capital. Their presidential entourage rode in nine automobiles.

When President Wilson dined at the Greyhound Inn in Forked River, he complimented the owner on the unique décor and admired his prize-winning greyhounds for which the inn was named.

THE CLAM CHOWDER CONTROVERSY

The Greyhound Inn was a popular place for decades as the Jersey Shore developed and the Barnegat Bay area grew. Manhattan clam chowder (made using tomatoes and "not necessarily associated with Manhattan") was a favorite dish served at the Greyhound Inn. In Andrew F. Smith's book *Souper Tomatoes*, he referred to *100 Summer and Winter Soups* (New York, 1943), in which author and soup expert Ann Roe Robbins praised the Greyhound Inn's Manhattan clam chowder. There was an ongoing debate as to whether the recipe with tomatoes could be considered true clam chowder. Some people insisted that creamy New England clam chowder was the only acceptable kind. New Jersey, with its resources of fresh, delicious tomatoes, served the Manhattan style in addition to the traditional New England chowder.

ATLANTIC CITY CLAM CHOWDER

Here's a century-old recipe that uses both tomatoes and milk in the chowder.

Chop 2 oz. of salt pork fine. Fry it a delicate brown in an iron kettle. Chop fine two dozen large clams. To the fried pork add the chopped clams, six medium sized tomatoes, two small carrots, one small onion, one cup of tomato pulp cut fine. Add one cup of liquor from the clams and water enough to keep from burning, more water may be added as it boils away, salt and pepper to taste. This chowder should be cooked slowly for at least two hours. Care must be taken to stir it often, so that it will not stick to the bottom of the kettle. Just before serving, add one pint of hot milk and a little parsley. Serve hot.

From Mrs. S.W. Hand's Cook Book of the Ladies Aid Society of the First Methodist Church, *Atlantic City, New Jersey. Special Collections and University Archives, Rutgers University Libraries.*

THE GHOST OF THE GREYHOUND INN

In the 1880s, the Parker House, a hotel owned by Sheriff Joseph Parker, occupied the Greyhound Inn site. Parker's daughter, Josephine, "suffered an untimely demise" there on October 10, 1893. Her spirit was said to haunt the site after the hotel was transformed into the Greyhound Inn. Guests and diners claimed to feel the eerie presence of Josephine.

In 1968, the Greyhound Inn was destroyed in a structure fire, and a pharmacy was later built on the site. Store employees reportedly saw doors open and close mysteriously. Late at night, workers stocking shelves claimed that objects moved on their own and that the phone would ring with no one on the line.[11] Was it Josephine? At the present time, the pharmacy is no longer there, and other businesses occupy the site; time will tell if the nineteenth-century ghost continues to play tricks.

AFTER THE WAR

By the beginning of World War I, the Jersey Shore had seen the "Age of Gluttony" fade. Many of the large old wooden seashore hotels had shut down or burned down. Wealthy people still ate at fine restaurants, but middle- and working-class vacationers were on the rise. They wanted good eats that were satisfying but reasonably priced. The foods they enjoyed and the restaurants they favored had become more casual.

During World War I, food was conserved, but food businesses picked up at the end of the conflict. When the soldiers returned from overseas, they brought new tastes with them. Ethnic restaurants gained in favor as immigrants poured into the country. Then, in 1920, the food and drink industry was significantly affected when the nation went dry. Prohibition and the Great Depression that followed brought many changes.

Today, many charming inns and fine restaurants are found at shore towns that have revived the ambiance of the Victorian era. Some of these establishments have been in business for generations; others are recently restored. At Cape May, the Peter Shields Inn, the Merion Inn and Aleathea's Restaurant are well known. In Bay Head, there's the historic Grenville Inn, and Beach Haven has The Gables. Spring Lake is home to The Breakers on the oceanfront and Whispers, an upscale restaurant housed in the historic Hewitt-Wellington Hotel.

Bounty from the Sea

FRESHNESS IS THE KEY

When the innovations of refrigeration and the swift transportation of food were in their infancy, the comforting thought of eating safe local seafood was a major attraction of a Jersey coast vacation. The Victorian hotels touted the freshness of their seafood. An 1880s menu from Leland's Ocean Hotel at Long Branch offered this reassuring statement: "The fish served are brought in morning and evening from the Ocean Hotel Fishery." Selections included sea bass, weak fish, black fish, blue fish, fish balls, stewed oysters and clam fritters…and these were on the *breakfast* menu. Besides seafood, you could order eggs, bread, grits, a variety of meats and fried Long Branch–style potatoes, as well as fruits and condiments. Beverage choices were coffee, tea, hot chocolate, milk and "Breakfast Wines."

MRS. MULFORD'S CLAM FRITTERS

Clam fritters were a simple but well-loved food on nineteenth-century menus, enjoyed either for breakfast or supper.

Make a batter as follows: two eggs well beaten, half cup sweet milk,[12] *flour enough to make stiff batter, to this add one pint chopped clams, well drained; beat all thoroughly and lastly before frying add one-quarter spoonful of soda; beat hard and fry in hot fat.*

From Cook Book of the YMCA of Asbury Park 1910, *Rutgers University Alexander Library Special Collections.*

A large array of local seafood was readily available along the Jersey coast—bass, bluefish, halibut, haddock, mackerel and flounder, as well as oysters, clams, crabs, scallops and lobsters. Fisheries or fish markets still exist but have become less prevalent in recent years. The kinds of fish available today have changed somewhat due to restrictions resulting from overfishing, as well as natural causes.

Most modern supermarkets have fresh seafood departments, but much of the fish sold is farmed, and many varieties come from faraway places. Some people still prefer the small specialty seafood markets, though even the smaller ones carry both local and out-of-the area fish. Then, of course, those who enjoy fishing may cook their own provided that the size and species are allowed.

Tastes do change. Some locally caught New Jersey seafood was particularly desirable during certain eras and not in others, such as American eels. Crispy fried eels are rarely seen on local restaurant menus anymore. Freshly caught eels were prevalent in the twentieth century, but they are now under consideration as an endangered species. The markets for eels today are found mostly in parts of Asia and Europe, where eel farms are in operation.

George Washington Fished Here

The profusion of fish on the Jersey coast's northernmost waters has realized rewards over the years for both professional and sport anglers. Looking back at the early history of fishing and local seafood, there are both factual accounts as well as "fish tales" that have been perpetuated. Just as it is today, you can't always believe what you read in the news. Old journals, logs, diaries, letters and newspapers are often all we have to try and piece together events of the past.

Many stories exist about English-born explorer Henry Hudson, who was working for the Dutch East India Company. He was searching for a passage to the Far East when his ship, the *Half Moon*, sailed along what is now the New Jersey shoreline. In 1609, Robert Juet, a ship's officer who kept a log, observed "many salmons, and mullets and rayes very great." According to Juet, some of the crew fished with a net and caught "10 great mullets, of a foot and a half long a piece, and a ray as great as four men could haul into the ship."[13]

In 1790, the first president of the United States fished along the Jersey coast near Sandy Hook. George Washington took a day sailer from New York, reportedly "for the benefit of the sea air and to amuse himself in the delightful re-creation of fishing." He was said to catch a "great number of seabass and black-fish."[14]

Toilers of the Sea

Both commercial and recreational sport fishing represent important industries along the Jersey coast. Commercial fishing is one of the most perilous jobs in the world. Improvements to safety have been made, but it remains a dangerous profession. In recent years, books, television reality shows, dramas and documentaries have increased public awareness of the dangers that seafaring families have always known. The New Jersey coast is treacherous, and its fishermen are constantly coping with the ever-changing weather and angry seas. Modern technology has helped, but they still face the same challenges as their predecessors so that fresh seafood can be on your table.

A charming illustration of the day after "one of the wildest storms of the season" was captioned: "A Pleasant December Day on the New Jersey Coast—Preparing the Lines for the Morrow's Fishing. A Scene at Galilee." *From* Frank Leslie's Illustrated Newspaper, *December 29, 1888.*

Bounty from the Sea

By the 1850s, sport fishermen were frequenting the stretch of barrier beach just south of Sandy Hook, where career fisherman lived at Nauvoo and Galilee. Some vacationers went there in the early nineteenth century for the fishing, and some simply enjoyed the salt air and beaches. Hotels began to open that provided accommodations and menus featuring the fresh catch of the day. Runs of bluefish prevailed, and hand-lining using lead squid was a popular way to snag them. Chronicler of the Jersey Shore Gustave Kobbe wrote about the fishermen at Seabright in 1888: "On the beach at Seabright, New Jersey, one can often witness an odd scene—a fleet of fishing skiffs under full sail and yet high and dry on the sand. They are the craft of the fishermen of Nauvoo, a quaint little settlement forming part of Seabright, inhabited entirely by toilers of the sea."

POUND FISHING

From the mid-1800s on, pound fishing was a way of life on the Jersey coast for many commercial fishermen. Huge nets were strung between poles off the beaches. The word "pound" referred to an enclosure created by the nets. Fish would be trapped when they wandered into the nets, and the men would go out to collect them, mostly in Sea Bright skiffs, similar to lifesaving boats. In the early days, horses were used to pull the boats onto the beach until they were replaced by electric motors. Long Branch, Belmar, Spring Lake and Long Beach Island had significant fish pound businesses. After the fish were hauled in, they were iced and shipped to market, many going to New York's Fulton Fish Market.

Woolley's Fish Market on Route 9 in Howell is a family-owned store that opened in 1960 but dates back to the pound fishing days a century ago. It spans four generations of a family working in the commercial fishing industry. Present owner John Woolley's grandfather began the business at Seaside Park in 1900. He moved it to Bradley Beach five years later and then to the Shark River area in 1944, when the tradition of selling fish on the beach ended.[15]

FAUX SARDINES

At Port Monmouth in the Bayshore area of Monmouth County, an impressive sardine fishery and cannery opened in 1874. Sardines—small, oily fish related to herrings—are named for Sardinia in the Mediterranean. Regarded as a "high-status" food in the nineteenth century, sardines were among the first available canned delicacies. Special sardine serving utensils and elegant glass or silver "sardine boxes" adorned Victorian dinner tables. Always well liked in Europe, sardines are experiencing popularity in the United States today, especially because they are known to be a tasty, heart-healthy food rich in omega-3 fatty acids.

The Port Monmouth sardine factory started out doing a brisk business. It caught its product off the shores of nearby Sandy Hook, and the sternwheeler *Orient* transported its canned "American sardines" to market. However, the company was shut down when it was found to be scamming the public. Its product was actually the menhaden, also known as mossbunker, normally used as fish bait and for fertilizer and not for human consumption.

A SHORE THING

The celebrated "shore dinner" seen on numerous Jersey Shore menus and in advertisements for more than a century seems to mean different things to different people. However, the phrase usually refers to a seafood dinner of fish (or lobster) accompanied by chicken and corn on the cob. The New Jersey "shore dinner" may be based on a similar New England dinner. In both regions, it's an undeniably good traditional meal served on the Atlantic Coast.

BAHRS LANDING: FROM NECKTIES TO SEAFOOD

The story of Bahrs Landing is the saga of a hardworking American family who built a successful food business at the Jersey Shore that has survived for generations. Although John Henry Bahrs (born in 1880) was from

Bahrs family group and guests in 1917. The Bahrs children are in the center row, Captain John H. Bahrs is on the right wearing a white hat and his wife, Flo, is next to him, with her hand under the chin of their son, John Jr. *Courtesy of Bahrs Landing.*

a seafaring family, his calling would be near the ocean but not on a ship. John Henry, known as "Jack," enlisted in the U.S. Marine Corps but soon received an honorable discharge due to an injury. He married Florence Ada, affectionately called "Flo." Jack's father-in-law reportedly worked as an oyster dealer in 1900, but Jack was not involved with the thriving oyster trade of the time; he worked as a garment cutter.

Men's haberdashery was a prosperous business in the early twentieth century. John Bahrs and Brothers was the name of the family necktie factory in Newark. Things were going well until an unfortunate turn of events when the tie factory was robbed. On Christmas Eve 1907, bolts of luxurious silk as well as finished neckties were stolen and could not readily be replaced. Months later, a career criminal named George "Humpty" Williams was captured and confessed to the crime.

By 1910, Jack and Flo were living on Newark's Walnut Street in the Tenth Ward and had a one-year-old son named John Alvin. The couple became disenchanted with urban living and wanted a fresh start. In 1913, they

COCKTAILS

Clam .... .35 Lobster .... .50
Tomato Juice .... .20
Grape Fruit Juice .... .15
Little Neck Clams on half shell, ½ doz. .... .35

SOUPS

Clam Chowder .... .25
Chicken Soup .... .25

STEAMED CLAMS 60c
With Broth   Drawn Butter
Bread and Butter
Order for Two 20c Extra

SHRIMP PLATTER — $1.00
Fried Florida Shrimp   Tartar Sauce
French Fried Potatoes   Salad
Bread and Butter

SHRIMP IN THE ROUGH — .55
Cocktail Sauce, Crackers

BROILED LOBSTER
$1.75 and Up
Butter Sauce
French Fried Potatoes

FLOUNDER PLATTER — $1.00
Fried Fillet of Flounder
French Fried Potatoes   Tartar Sauce
Salad
Bread and Butter

COMBINATION SEA FOOD PLATTER
$1.25
Assorted Sea Food
French Fried Potatoes   Salad
Bread and Butter

FRESH SCALLOP PLATTER — $1.10
Fried Deep Sea Scallops, Tartar Sauce
French Fried Potatoes

SUGGESTIONS

BROILED SEA BASS PLATTER.....1.50
F.F. POT. VEG. & SALAD

BROILED STRIPED BASS PLATTER..1.90

BROILED SEA TROUT PLATTER......1.00

SOFT SHELL CRAB PLATTER.........1.25

LET. TOM. & BACON SAND...........40

SHREWSBURY RIVER CLAM PLATTER
$1.00
Fried Clams   French Fried Potatoes
Tartar Sauce
Bread and Butter

SALADS

Shrimp $1.25
Lobster 1.50
Lettuce and Tomato .... .40

SANDWICHES

Special Fish Sandwich .... .50
Swiss Cheese .... .30
Lettuce, Tomato and Bacon .... .35 ⁴
Fried Shrimp .... .60
Ham .... .25

BEVERAGES
Tea 10c   Coffee 10c   Milk 10c
Iced Coffee 15c   Iced Tea 15c

DESSERT — .15

Check out the depression-era prices on this 1930s menu from Bahrs Landing. It offered unpretentious but tasty fresh seafood, as well as other selections. *Courtesy of Bahrs Landing.*

decided to leave Newark and seek a new life in a quieter area. They ended up in Highlands, a small maritime community in Monmouth County across the Shrewsbury River from Sandy Hook. They purchased Allie Miller's, a boat rental business near the Highlands Bridge, and ran it for the next few years. Then they acquired McGuire's, a beached houseboat (also near the bridge) that catered to sport fishermen with rooms to let, a restaurant and boats for hire.

In 1917, just one day after Jack and Flo signed the contracts to buy the place, a nor'easter destroyed all of the rowboats. So they focused on serving

"The Founder's Table." Grandfather Jack Bahrs is enjoying a lobster dinner in 1951. The powder room had been moved but not the sign. It is said that he dined at this little table every night. Either the servers really liked him or this was posed. *Courtesy of Bahrs Landing.*

meals to the fisherman who were staying there. Jack and Flo did the cooking and made hearty breakfasts of fried eels, buckwheat pancakes and fresh eggs. For lunches and dinners, they offered stews, fresh fish and Jack's famous clam chowder. The couple now had four young children—John Jr. (Bud), Al, Ken and Ruth—who helped their parents and learned how to run the business as they grew.

During the Great Depression, the restaurant fared well, with Bud Bahrs and his wife, Peg, running the business. People enjoyed the reasonably priced quality seafood. They stayed close to home when they could not afford travel to faraway destinations.

Customers came by boat, by automobile and by train. Although no longer in existence, a branch of the Central Jersey Railroad went from Hoboken through Highlands and down the coast to Long Branch, with Bahrs Landing as one of the stops. Their food became so popular that they eventually needed more room, so they jacked up the beach house and bulkheaded the property to accommodate more customers. In the mid-1950s, the upstairs motel rooms were turned into offices.

Bahrs Special

This creamy seafood mix that Bahrs served in clamshells is from the years when Bud and Peg ran the restaurant.

½ pound cooked king crab meat
½ pound boiled scallops
½ pound cooked shrimp, coarsely chopped
½ pound lump crabmeat
2 tablespoons minced Spanish or Bermuda onion
1 cup melted butter
⅔ cup flour
2 cups milk
½ teaspoon white pepper
2 tablespoons salt
1 cup Sauterne wine
½ cup whipped heavy cream

First prepare Supreme Sauce: sauté onions lightly in butter, add flour and cream well, then add milk, pepper, salt and wine. Cook over slow heat until thickened. Set aside ½ cup of sauce and add to it whipped cream to be used as topping. Mix all seafood with balance of sauce and serve in large clamshells. Cover with topping and bake for 12 minutes at 350 degrees, or until brown. Serves 6–8.

Courtesy of Bahrs Landing.

In 1974, Bud and Peg retired from the business. The expanded restaurant, which retains the historic ambiance and reputation for good food, is owned by Ray Cosgrove and his son, Jay Cosgrove, the fourth-generation great-grandson of the founders. They have made many improvements and added Moby's Outside Deck & Lobster Pound. In the main restaurant, there's a gift shop, as well as displays of vintage photos, model boats and seafaring memorabilia. The "dock and dine" facilities are popular with boaters. Bahrs Landing is a historical landmark and one of the oldest continually family-run restaurants in the United States.

THE OYSTER CRAZE

Although oysters are frequently listed as appetizers or bar food today, in the late nineteenth and early twentieth centuries, the coveted "pearls of the sea" were far more prevalent as both starters and main courses on menus. The ancient Romans ate oysters, and the mollusk's gastronomic history goes so far back that no one can pinpoint exactly when they were first eaten by man. It is said that coastal Native Americans included them in their diet thousands of years ago. From colonial times through the early nineteenth century, oysters were common tavern fare and street food sold in stalls or vendors' carts in Boston, New York, Philadelphia and other cities. At the New Jersey Shore's Victorian hotels and restaurants, oysters on the half shell were popular starters, but it didn't stop there. Oysters were served in a wide variety of ways.

Cream of Oyster Soup

The popular New Jersey oyster sometimes found its way onto menus in the form of soup. In 1847, two New Jersey brothers, John and Adam Exton (Trenton), developed the oyster cracker. It was hailed as the perfect accompaniment to oyster soup.

2 pints oysters
1 quart half-and-half cream, or 2 cups milk and 2 cups heavy cream
$\frac{1}{2}$ teaspoon marjoram
1 celery rib with leaves
1 teaspoon salt
$\frac{1}{2}$ teaspoon white pepper
2 tablespoons butter

Heat the oysters in their own liquor until their edges begin to curl but no longer or the oysters will toughen. Heat the cream with the marjoram and celery until it simmers. Strain it into the pan with the oysters and their liquor. Season with salt and white pepper. Heat but do not boil. Serve in hot bowls with a teaspoon of butter on each serving.

From The Victorian Seaside Cookbook. *Courtesy of the New Jersey Historical Society.*

By the close of the nineteenth century, oyster houses and lobster palaces in New York City were all the rage, and similar establishments had opened up across the country. East Coast oysters were shipped in ice to western destinations. According to author John Mariani, "Americans had become oyster mad. Annual consumption was 660 oysters per person, against 120 in the United Kingdom and only 26 in France."[16]

Maryland, New York, Virginia and New Jersey were the states that reaped the greatest profits from oysters. The industry was thriving all along the Jersey coast, but several areas were key producers. Cape May County was an important oystering area, and the Maurice River Cove on the Delaware was famous for its oysters. The small towns of this interesting area, sometimes called "the other Jersey Shore," have names such as Bivalve and Shellpile (Cumberland County). An excellent source of recipes and food history for this region can be found in *Down Jersey Cooking: Celebrating Our Heritage from Past to Present* by Joe Colanero.

At the northern shore, the oyster industry was located mainly in Perth Amboy and Keyport, as well as at other ports in the Bayshore area. Along the Navesink and Shrewsbury Rivers, towns that had profitable oyster businesses included Rumson, Fair Haven, Little Silver, Oceanport and Red Bank. The demand for oysters was so great that it wasn't long before many natural oyster beds were used up. By 1892, three quarters of the seed oysters were from the Chesapeake Bay area of Maryland and from Virginia."[17]

Much of the shellfish sold today in New Jersey is farm-raised, as shellfish populations have diminished due to overharvesting. Aquaculture is a sustainable alternative that was used in New Jersey more than a century ago. A Rutgers biologist named Julius Nelson pioneered oyster aquaculture at his laboratory in Tuckerton during the late nineteenth century. After his death, his son, Thurlow, took over, and by the 1950s, Harold Haskin was running the labs and researching the farming of hard clams and disease-resistant oysters. Today, the state and dedicated environmental groups are working to restore shellfish to Jersey Shore waters.

THE HISTORIC SITE OF SALT CREEK GRILLE

On the banks of the Navesink River, there's evidence of clam and oyster shells believed to have been left by Native Americans before white settlers arrived. In Rumson near the Oceanic Bridge, today's popular Salt Creek Grille was preceded by several historic eateries. In the mid-1800s, a busy steamboat dock used for both passengers and freight was located at the foot of Washington Street. Thomas G. Hunt, a steamboat owner, opened a hotel and annex in 1845 to cash in on the increasing flow of visitors. The establishment changed names over the years and was known as Hunt's Pavilion Hotel, the Shrewsbury Inn and the Rumson Inn.

In 1891, the dock was relocated a block west to make way for the bridge. A new bridge, completed in 1940, replaced the outdated and precarious Victorian one. During the 1940s, the Rumson Inn, owned by Jack Madden, was located in the annex. Both the old hotel and annex were demolished in 1960, and the River House restaurant was built. It later became known as Fisherman's Wharf until it was closed in 1996. The property's current owner is Rumson Management Company. In 1998, Steve Bidgood opened Salt Creek Grille and continues to operate and maintain the restaurant. Today, the stunning Craftsman-style eatery, with its mesquite grill, thrives next to the recently refurbished Oceanic Bridge. The mighty steamboats are long gone, but the view remains spectacular.

DOCK'S OYSTER HOUSE: A VICTORIAN SURVIVOR

A celebrated Atlantic City restaurant from the Victorian era is Dock's Oyster House at 2405 Atlantic Avenue. It has been continuously in operation since 1897 in the tradition of a classic seafood and steak eatery. Oyster madness was in full swing during the Gay Nineties, and the resort city was *the* place for fashionable ladies and gents to vacation. The Boardwalk was lined with big old wood-frame hotels, and rolling chairs were a recent innovation. A man

When it first opened in 1897, Dock's Oyster House in Atlantic City was a "storefront" restaurant. In business today at the same location on Atlantic Avenue, it's greatly updated but hasn't lost its Victorian charm. *Courtesy of Frank Dougherty.*

named Harry ("Call me 'Dock'") Dougherty decided that it was a good time to open a restaurant, and he chose a location off the Boardwalk on Atlantic Avenue. With no liquor license but a reputation for quality food, Dock's kept open through such hard times as World War I and the Great Depression.

In 1938, Harry's health was failing, so he turned the restaurant over to his son, Joseph, who ran the place until he was called to active duty in World War II. Joe's wife, Anne, kept the business going during the war years. When Joe returned in 1945, the couple enlarged the restaurant from sixty to eighty seats. Dock's continued to flourish until the "Queen of Resorts" suffered an economic downturn during the late 1960s.

Joseph retired and passed the business on to his son, Joe Jr., a man with a vision and the perseverance to make it work. He totally remodeled the interior, expanded the seating capacity to twice its original size, and obtained a liquor license. The next decade was a tough one, but Joe persisted, and his wife, Arleen, and their sons pitched in and helped to keep the restaurant going while glitzy new casinos were opening during the 1980s. Joe died in 1999, and his youngest son, Frank, took over the reins. With the help of his mother and Joe III, Dock's was remodeled again in 2001 and a full raw bar added.

Today, Dock's is truly a piece of Jersey Shore culinary history. For even more "oyster madness," the Doughertys opened Harry's Oyster Bar and Seafood in the courtyard of the former historic Dennis Hotel, now Bally's, in 2011. The boardwalk restaurant preserves traditions of the old oyster houses but with flatscreens in the sports bar, something the Victorians probably would have relished. (Frank Dougherty and his wife, Maureen Shay, also own Atlantic City's historic Knife and Fork Inn.)

HACKNEY'S AND STARN'S:
THE ATLANTIC CITY MAMMOTHS

If a trivia game question asked what the world's most famous seafood restaurants were, Hackney's and Captain Starn's would be good answers. Both of these huge eateries were located at the inlet area of Atlantic City and had their heydays in the 1940s and 1950s. The inlet was the last stop on the old trolley line and the place where the trolley cars turned around. During prohibition, the inlet was known as a haven for bootleggers to bring in the "hooch."

One of Harry Hackney's most successful gimmicks was the lobster pool at his Atlantic City restaurant. You could choose your own that would be cooked especially for you. This view is from the 1930s, but the purification tanks were there for decades.

Captain Starn's restaurant on the inlet at Atlantic City operated excursion boats like this one, as well as sailboats. This souvenir folder cover is from the early 1950s. Some people said that owner Captain Starn looked like President Dwight D. Eisenhower.

In 1912, Harry Hackney opened up a clam stand on the boardwalk at the inlet that just grew and grew. Owner Hackney had great marketing skills and even constructed a fishing pier across from his restaurant so customers could fish, a feature dubbed "fishing from the window." He expanded the place, which was a summer-only restaurant until 1926, and added a vast addition in 1929, advertising that the restaurant could seat 3,200 people and was open year round.

Using his ability as a showman, Harry Hackney boasted that his restaurant "was as famous as the Boardwalk" and lured celebrities there over the years. Al Smith, governor of New York in the 1920s, is said to have originated one of Hackney's favorite slogans, "Eat them where they're caught." Silent film stars Tom Mix, Mae Murray, Douglas Fairbanks, "America's Sweetheart" Mary Pickford and countless entertainers, sports stars and politicians ate at Hackney's.

The place was rebuilt after damage from the hurricane of 1944. Harry Hackney died the following year, but his son and then grandson continued the restaurant. Hackney's burned down in 1963, was rebuilt and was opened again two years later. It didn't do well and was shut down permanently in the early 1980s as the new casinos opened. The inlet area went into a state of decline, but it is flourishing once again today.

Sea lions barking for fish welcomed customers to Captain Starn's Restaurant and Boating Center at Main and Caspian Avenues. In 1940, Captain Clarence Starn, with experience operating tourist boats since the 1920s, opened a restaurant at the inlet near Hackney's at the site of the old Hyman's restaurant that dated back to the nineteenth century. Captain Starn's wasn't just about eating; it was also about entertainment. At Starn's pier, both powerboats and sailboats provided fun outings. Deep-sea fishing trips were offered, and a seaplane took gutsy tourists for a thrilling ride. For the "faint of heart," it featured a quaint wishing well surrounded by a small garden and gift shops. Starn's caught much of its own seafood and had a lobster pool similar to Hackney's, as well as an on-site fish market. There were several bars, including one on a yacht. Customer photos printed on matchbook covers and in souvenir folders provided lasting memories for families. The captain's nephew, Clarence "Skeets" Apel, ran the excursion part of the business.

After Captain Clarence Starn's death in 1969, the place kept going for about ten years, but Atlantic City's inlet area kept losing tourists. Starn's was razed in 1992.

Another famous restaurant at the inlet, popular in the 1940s and 1950s, was Carson's Triangle. It is well remembered for its crunchy French fried lobster tails, a specialty, and its fried shrimp. Though casinos were not built on the once bustling sites of these legendary restaurants at the scenic inlet, the area is experiencing a resurgence today of housing, shops and eateries. But the barking sea lions and women dressed as lobsters are history.

FISH ON WHEELS

If you couldn't get to the fishery, the fishery would come to you! Fishmongers in the early days had horse-drawn wagons to peddle their wares along the Jersey coast, but by the early 1920s, motorized trucks were being used.

As more people acquired automobiles and gained mobility, the trucks were not needed. Fish markets and restaurants dotted the Jersey Shore and flourished at most every resort town. In 1924, Ollie Klein Sr. began to sell fish from his truck throughout Asbury Park, Ocean Grove and the Neptune area. Four years later, he rented a retail seafood store on Fifth Avenue in Belmar. A year later, in 1929, Ollie opened Klein's Fish Market at 708 River Road on the Shark River in Belmar.

Ollie soon built a little addition to the market with a stove, where his wife, Elizabeth, would make clam chowder and fish sandwiches for her family. The fish market customers would sniff the tantalizing aroma of her cooking, and this gave Ollie the idea to open a restaurant, with "Lizzie" as the chef. But that never happened, as her priority was to care for their children, Ollie Jr., John (Jack) and Jeanette.

In the 1930s and 1940s, Ollie operated both the retail fish market and a wholesale market, shipping the local catch to New York's Fulton Fish Market. He trained his sons to work in the fish business, and they joined him full time after World War II. Ollie Jr. and Jack worked with their dad throughout the 1950s. Young Ollie Klein III learned the seafood business in the early 1960s while working at the market during his high school and college years. After their father died in 1972, Ollie Jr. and Jack took over. Ollie III learned about the restaurant business while working as general manager of a well-known local seafood eatery. In 1990, after the passing of Jack Klein, Ollie III returned to work at the family market. Today, he runs the establishment that is at the same location but is greatly expanded and known as Ollie Klein's Fish Market, Waterside Café, Grill Room & Sushi Bar.

A picturesque postcard dated 1905 depicts a pound boat crew coming in with their daily net catch at Long Branch.

As one of his many publicity stunts, Atlantic City restaurateur Harry Hackney posed with his pretty "lobster waitresses" in the 1940s.

Photos of restaurant interiors usually feature empty tables, but it's more fun to see the people. A 1950s Atlantic City postcard provides a look at Hackney's customers. Many of them are wearing the proverbial lobster bibs. The long, open kitchen is visible in the back.

Shapely "Jersey girls" competed for the title of "Miss Seafood Princess" at Point Pleasant Beach as part of the Big Sea Day festivities in the 1950s and early 1960s.

Fresh New Jersey clams displayed at the Lusty Lobster seafood market in Highlands.

Eatmor was a cooperative that started in 1907 and ended in the early 1950s. Its berries came from New Jersey, Wisconsin and Massachusetts. The crate labels, such as this one with stunning graphics, are no longer in use and have become popular collectibles.

In the nineteenth century, tomatoes were called "love apples." Look carefully to spot the differences between these two E.C. Hazard labels. There was a series of these; each variety of tomato was paired with a different flower. Hazard was famous for his ketchup factory in Shrewsbury. *Courtesy of the Shrewsbury Historical Society.*

The Heinz Pier in Atlantic City provided an elegant showplace for food products developed by Henry J. Heinz of Pittsburgh. Opened in 1898, the pier featured "Heinz's 57 Varieties," including ketchup and pickles. The hurricane of 1944 destroyed the pier, and it was not rebuilt.

The Sickles seasonal farm stand in Little Silver as it appeared in this 1982 postcard hadn't changed much since it began in the 1940s. Today, it's the sumptuous Sickles Market, which still sells produce but also gourmet foods, plants, baked goods and gifts. Bob Sickles Sr. still farms some blackberries, beets, corn and other produce. His son, Bob Jr., runs the year-round store, which features many exciting events.

The beauty of Jersey blues! The blueberry was first cultivated at Whitesbog in Burlington County. The official state fruit of New Jersey, blueberries are a popular food to eat all along the Jersey Shore.

Succulent and sweet, Jersey corn is a favorite vegetable among young and old. Munching corn on the cob is a shore tradition. It's been served at Victorian hotel dinners, beach picnics, clambakes and restaurants.

Jersey Shore peaches are famous! This yummy fresh peach cake made with them is from a 1949 New Jersey homemaker's recipe. It could be called a "peach upside down cake."

In the 1930s, Tory's, owned by a Japanese couple, was a popular West Long Branch restaurant until a tragic turn of events shut it down. It went through several changes of ownership, and today it's the site of Branches, an upscale banquet hall and catering facility.

When prohibition was repealed in 1933, bars opened up to great fanfare. In Atlantic City, the Ritz Carlton featured the Merry-Go-Round Bar. Atlantic City's celebrated political boss Nucky Johnson was a regular customer.

An original watercolor by Marie Natale, *Summer Sisters of the Chalfonte Kitchen* portrays the hotel cooks at Cape May's Victorian gingerbread treasure, the Chalfonte. Chef Helen Dickerson (1909–1990), famous for her southern dishes, is depicted both as her younger self cutting a pie and some years later, gazing out at the viewer. Her daughters, who still cook at the Chalfonte, are by the stove, and on the left is a former owner of the hotel, Ann LeDuc. *Courtesy of Marie Natale.*

The Circus Drive-In on Route 35 in Wall Township, an independent restaurant that's still in business, has expanded but appears much the same as it did in this late 1950s photo. Innovative menu items have included "Trapeze Treat" and "Three Ring Circus Delight." Usually, the parking lot is packed with cars.

A multiview 1970s postcard of Ed Zaberer's restaurant in Wildwood. The classic family restaurant that began in the 1950s was kitschy yet stylish and was famous for humongous portions. Ed's brother, Charlie, owned a restaurant, also called Zaberer's, on the Black Horse Pike, near Atlantic City. Both establishments are gone now.

One of Maruca's signature "swirly tomato pies" at Seaside Park.

Although this photo is from 2012, the legendary White House Subs on Arctic Avenue in Atlantic City looks almost exactly as it did when it opened in 1946. It's a must for tourists, and the walls are covered with photos of celebrities who ate here.

A vintage linen postcard of Max's Famous Hot Dogs, established in 1928, shows the location of the renowned eatery's first shop on the Long Branch Boardwalk.

Celia Maybaum of Max's Famous Hot Dogs has hobnobbed with dozens of celebrities who've eaten at her Long Branch restaurant. She's seen here with the Jersey Shore's own superstar, Bruce Springsteen, in the 1990s. *Courtesy of Max's Famous Hot Dogs.*

The landmark WindMill on Ocean Avenue in Long Branch is the first and only one of the small chain's restaurants that is actually in the shape of a windmill. The little deck upstairs has been a favorite spot to eat since the building opened in 1964.

A chili cheese dog, oozing with flavor, from the WindMill at Long Branch.

A whimsical 1920s advertisement for Fralinger's Salt Water Taffy features a couple perched atop a giant candy box on the Atlantic City Beach.

At Wildwood-by-the-Sea, Sagel's was a popular store that sold salt water taffy, Huyler's Chocolates and other sweet treats. This postcard is from the early twentieth century. The store burned down in the Christmas Day fire of 1943.

A vintage image of a Fralinger's Salt Water Taffy store.

This colorful frozen custard stand belonging to Kohr's The Original, established in 1919, is located on the Seaside Heights Boardwalk at Grant Avenue by the Casino Pier, 2012 photo.

A vintage-looking sign for Kohr's The Original at Seaside Heights. The iconic orange and vanilla swirly cone is probably the most recognizable of all its delicious frozen custard treats.

THE PEANUT STORE
1011 BOARDWALK, ATLANTIC CITY, N. J.

The reverse of this 1940s linen postcard reads, "When in Atlantic City, visit The Peanut Store, the Home of Mr. Peanut, where world-famous Planters Peanuts are sold. See Planters Peanuts roasted right before your eyes and mail them to your friends back home." The store no longer exists, but the peanuts do!

The author and her grandkids are enjoying ice cream cones. The beach, arcade games, rides, miniature golf and some yummy treats…a perfect day at the Jersey Shore in 2012.

Ollie Klein Jr. and his sister, Jeanette, on the running board of their dad's fish truck in 1927. Ollie Sr. peddled fresh fish throughout Belmar, Asbury Park, Neptune and Ocean Grove from 1924 to 1928. *Courtesy of Klein's Fish Market.*

In 1929, Ollie Klein opened this airy Belmar seafood market. *From left to right*: Dave Sanderson, Ollie Klein Sr. and Pete Olsen. The market is now the updated Klein's Fish Market and Waterside Café. *Courtesy of Klein's Fish Market.*

DAVE AND EVELYN'S

In the early days of the fish market, Dave Sanderson worked with Ollie Klein but soon left to open his own business. With Evelyn Longstreet, he sold clams during the Great Depression from a little stand by the F Street Bridge. Later, they opened the Original Dave and Evelyn's seafood eatery. The restaurant, popular in the 1950s and 1960s, was located on the west side of F Street and Fifth Avenue near the bridge, close to where they had operated their clam stand. (This later became the site of a Jack Baker's Lobster Shanty and then Amici's Restaurant, which opened in 1999.) For a while, Dave had his own seafood restaurant at 700 F Street, but it was never as popular as the main restaurant, and it shut down in the 1970s.

THE HISTORIC PORT OF CAPE MAY

Schellenger's Landing was named for a seventeenth-century family of whalers who came from New England in the 1600s to settle in South Jersey. In the 1800s, this was the only outlet to Cape May Island for commercial fishing boats and steamboats that carried tourists. Cape May Harbor was built to open up the waterways so that the larger boats could enter.

Cape May is said to be the second busiest port on the eastern seaboard for offloading seafood today, after New Bedford, Massachusetts. With its gingerbread gems and pristine gardens enclosed by picket fences, the downtown area of Cape May is nothing like the dock area. There's Victorian Cape May, and there's seafaring Cape May—both are of historic importance.

The Lobster House, on Fisherman's Wharf in Cape May, has been in operation since the early 1950s and continuously owned by the Laudeman family. Wally and Marijane, the parents of current owner Keith Laudeman, established the restaurant. Going back even further, Keith's grandfather, Jess, started a wholesale fish business in the 1920s. In those days, a railroad track came right up to Schellenger's Landing, and the catch could be loaded directly onto a train and delivered to city markets. The Laudemans' fishing enterprise is called the Cold Spring Fish and Supply Company. Keith, once a commercial fisherman, joined the family business in the 1980s. Although the restaurant was devastated by a raging fire in 1964, and another fire in 2006 damaged outer buildings but not the dining areas, the Lobster House stayed in operation and never lost its popularity or salty charm.

Owner Wally Laudeman of the Lobster House in Cape May is bartending at his restaurant during the 1950s. The popular nautical-themed eatery is greatly expanded and enjoyed by diners today. *Courtesy of the Lobster House.*

The splendid schooner *American*, berthed alongside the Lobster House in Cape May, circa 1965, continues to be a popular venue for cocktails before having a delicious fresh seafood dinner. *Courtesy of the Lobster House.*

Permanently moored alongside the Lobster House's main dining room is a 130-foot Grand Banks sailing vessel used as an outdoor dining area. The schooner *American* has been a feature at the Lobster House since 1965 and provides a pleasurable setting for enjoying cocktails and outdoor dining. The décor inside the main restaurant is traditional and nautical in style, the lobby walls are covered with historic photos and the wait staff wear crisp retro uniforms. Most importantly of all, the varied menu features seafood that is fresh and fabulous.

The Cape May area is a top producer of scallops, and the Laudemans own six commercial scallop boats. They also operate a fish market that's adjacent to the restaurant. Following is a tasty recipe from the Lobster House.

Cape May Scallops
(wrapped in bacon with a horseradish dipping sauce)

A Lobster House specialty.

8 oz. scallops
1 lime, "juice only"
bacon, "blanched 4 to 5 minutes"
salt and black pepper, "lite sprinkle"
2 tbs. olive oil

HORSERADISH DIPPING SAUCE
4 oz. sour cream
1 oz. horseradish
1 tsp. chopped chives "fresh or dried"
mix together and chill for 20 minutes

In mixing bowl add scallops, lime juice, olive oil, salt and pepper. Lightly toss. Grill scallops 1 minute each side and remove from grill. Wrap scallops in bacon, secure with a long toothpick and put in oven 375 for about 5 minutes or until scallops are cooked thru. Drizzle plate with horseradish sauce and place scallops on plate. Ready to serve.

Courtesy of the Lobster House, Cape May.

"What's Cooking":
Long Beach Island in the 1950s

In the early 1950s, Long Beach Island experienced rapid growth with increasing numbers of both summer sojourners and permanent residents. New businesses were opening up, and although there were plenty of restaurants, many people enjoyed cooking fish they caught or those they purchased at the island fisheries. A local weekly paper, the *Beachcomber* (still published today), ran a delightful column called "What's Cooking?" by Lorelei Phinney. The writer with the intriguing pen name was LBI's own Josephine Thomas, author of the Great Depression story *Fisherman's Wife*.[18] She extended an open invitation for island cooks to submit their favorite recipes, as well as their "tips and tricks on fish cookery."

With a breezy flair, Lorelei dished out practical advice to her readers: "How can you tell a fresh fish from a stale one? Not by aroma alone, you can be sure. You will know if your purchase is fresh if: its eyes are bright, clear, full and bulging; its gills are reddish pink, free of slime or odor; its flesh is firm and springs back when pressed, never separating from the bones; its scales are bright and cling tightly to the skin."

Local clams came in three sizes: cherrystone and little necks for eating on the half shell and chowders for use in cooking. Regarding their availability, Lorelei said that you could buy them from dealers like Joe Lafferty on the causeway or reputable fisheries, or with a license, you could rake in your own. She described the way to shuck them:

Rinse clams in cold water and scrub those that don't appear absolutely clean of bay mud and grit. Place clam in palm of left hand with point or hinged part against palm. Lay blade of thin strong and sharp knife between broad front of shells (ask your hardware dealer for a clam-opening knife) between broad front of shells. Clamp all four fingers tightly over knife and exert pressure forcing blade between shells, then twisting knife entire length of shell until tough muscle is severed and clam opens. Pry shells apart and free clam on all sides. If you are making chowder, open clams over bowl and strain broth to be used with the chowder. If not, chill broth and reserve as appetizer for your sea food dinner.

Lorelei thought that "a purely sissy way" to pry open clams is to steam them or to put them in the oven and bake them open: "Not only is this to be deplored from a purely sporting outlook, but naturally, it toughens the meat of the clam and makes your ultimate dish less succulent."

Enthusiastic readers responded to Lorelei's "What's Cooking?" request and contributed favorite recipes, such as this one from Mrs. Harry Staton of Harvey Cedars.

Baked Blue Fish with Barnegat Sauce

Select a large fish (bonita, mackerel or blue), three pounds or more; have it split and the center bone removed. Place in greased baking dish, skin side down. Dot generously with margarine and bake in a 400 degree oven for 15 minutes. Spread on Barnegat Sauce in a thick layer and bake 20 minutes or longer. For a small fish, allow slightly less time; for a five or six pounder, about five minutes more—or until the meat flakes easily when tested with a fork.

BARNEGAT SAUCE
1 cup thickened canned or fresh stewed tomatoes
1 heaping tbs. mayonnaise
1 tsp. capers
1 tbs. minced parsley
¼ tsp. oregano (or basil)
breadcrumbs

Thicken tomatoes by melting 1½ tablespoons margarine and blending in 1½ tablespoons of flour. Add tomatoes and stir over low heat until slightly thickened. Remove from heat and add mayonnaise, capers, parsley and oregano or basil. Add enough breadcrumbs to give a creamy, but not pasty, consistency. Spread over fish as directed above. The sauce may be prepared in advance and kept in the refrigerator until it is time to bake the fish.

Twinkle, Twinkle Little Starfish

The sea star or starfish is a cherished icon for décor, jewelry or various seashore souvenirs, and it has been romanticized in literature. Dried starfish (not really a fish; it is *Ichthyophagous echinoderm*) are fun finds for beachcombers, who take them home. But would you want to see fresh ones on the menu at a seafood restaurant or cook them for dinner? The starfish feeds on mollusks and is rarely used as food for people. In her column, Josephine Thomas expressed disbelief when she heard that members of the Gourmet Society of Lower Barnegat Bay had discussed making a recipe for starfish! So, she decided to research the topic.

When oyster madness was sweeping the nation, oyster growers were deeply concerned about an increase in starfish, which were eating their harvests and destroying their profits. Starfish were considered to be pesky creatures on the same level as flies, mosquitoes and fleas. Man was considered to be the worst enemy of the oyster, with starfish coming in as a close second. Eliminating the starfish proved to be difficult because even when cut or smashed, their arms can regenerate and turn into more starfish.

In the 1880s, Thomas J. Murray, the author of *Salads and Sauces*, wrote: "A happy thought occurred…perhaps the star-fish might be utilized as a food, and if he could once be forced into that new position the popular demand for him might do much toward restraining the threatening multiplication of his kind." Murray praised the starfish for its cleanliness and plumpness from feeding on oysters. He concocted starfish bisque but found it hard to get anyone to try it. His favorite recipe will be skipped here, although Lorelei did include two of Murray's recipes in "What's Cooking?" Interesting reading, but it's doubtful that any LBI vacationers actually made them (I hope they didn't). Starfish are not on Jersey Shore menus today and not recommended for eating. However, there are some types that are considered delicacies in Japan.

Excerpts from "What's Cooking" are courtesy of Margaret Thomas Buchholz, daughter of Josephine Thomas ("Lorelei Phinney").

An Old Clothes Washer for Cooking Lobsters

The son of a New Jersey fisherman, Jack Baker learned about the sea from his father. After finishing high school, Jack went to Florida to deliver a boat and decided to take a job as a busboy at a major hotel. Here Jack first discovered that he had talent as a chef. He met his wife in Florida, and after a few years, they went to New Jersey and lived at Point Pleasant Beach. Then Jack entered the service, his tour of duty ending in 1955. He then returned to the Jersey Shore, where he fished with his father.

Soon, Jack and his wife opened a tiny restaurant with only four tables on the side porch of their home. Jack and his father would cook the lobsters they caught in an old clothes washer that had been converted to a gas-fired cooker. Soon, people were clamoring to eat their fresh lobsters. Their business grew and grew, and the old clothes washer was traded in for a bathtub, which was also converted to a gas-fired cooker. "The porch could no longer accommodate everyone, so a building was constructed on what now is the present site of the Lobster Shanty. Yes, this was the very first Jack Baker's Lobster Shanty."[19] The business continued to expand, and updated lobster cookers replaced the old makeshift ones. Jack Baker's Lobster Shanty and Wharfside is known as "the place that seafood lovers (like you!) made famous."

Today, Jack Baker's Lobster Shanty is part of Chefs International, which also operates restaurants in Toms River and in Florida at Cocoa Beach and Vero Beach.

Miss Seafood Princess

At Point Pleasant Beach in the 1950s and 1960s, a popular pageant was held each August during the "Big Sea Day" festivities to crown a "Miss Seafood Princess." Although people figured that it was an event to promote the seafood industry, former Mayor Jack Sinn (1957–61) explained that it really had nothing to do with food.[20] The pageant didn't compare to the magnitude of Atlantic City's Miss America, but the parade and contest were very popular. Richard M. Nixon and his family sometimes attended the event while visiting their summer home at Mantoloking during Nixon's years as vice president.

An amusing anecdote about the 1959 Miss Seafood Princess, Susan Millstein, appeared in papers across the nation. In her first public announcement, she openly admitted, "I guess I should say I like fish but I just don't and I won't eat it. The only time I went fishing I fell into Silver Lake [Belmar] trying to make a cast."

TRADITIONAL VERSUS NEW

In the mid-twentieth century, a seafood eatery called Doris and Ed's on Bay Avenue in Highlands was a popular spot, serving traditional favorites such as fried fish platters and whole lobsters. It offered quality food, but the menu didn't include innovative or creative dishes. All that changed in 1978 when Chef Jim Filip purchased the restaurant. Filip drew inspiration from the French-born chef Gilbert LeCoze, who ran Le Bernadin in Manhattan until his untimely death in 1994. LeCoze was famous for his "revolutionary approach" to seafood dishes. Likewise, Filip wanted to change the way Americans perceive seafood; his vision was to bring exquisite flavors and excitement to the Monmouth County Shore. Filip, a master chef and connoisseur of fine wines, added panache to the outdated Doris and Ed's.

Under Filip's ownership, Doris and Ed's was the first New Jersey restaurant to receive the coveted James Beard Award of Excellence as an "America's Regional Classic." The restaurant has been featured in publications including *Gourmet*, *Bon Appétit* and the *New York Times* and on the Food Network. Jim Filip's renowned wine list was awarded the Wine Spectator's Award of Excellence for many years.

After damage from a hurricane in 2011, Filip felt that it was time to retire, and the restaurant will not be reopening. It's now a slice of Jersey Shore food history to be savored. Following is one of Filip's inventive recipes for a local fish.

Crisp Black Sea Bass with Broccoli Rabe, Chorizo Hash, Jersey Clams and Saffron Cream

4 8-oz. black sea bass filets
3 oz. basil
8 oz. canola oil
20 little neck clams
½ cup white wine
2 shallots
1–2 tsp. saffron
1 qt. heavy cream

2 lbs. Idaho potatoes
1 bunch broccoli rabe
4 links chorizo sausage
5 cloves garlic
4 tbsp. sweet butter
2 cherry tomatoes
chervil for garnish
salt and pepper

Scale and filet black bass. Score skin and place paper towel on skin to dry. Blanch basil in boiling water and chill-wring dry. Place in blender with salt and pepper and 2 oz. canola oil, then blend. Strain through cheesecloth. Peel and mince shallots.

Steam clams in white wine and shallots, just until open, remove clams from their shells and set aside covered. Keep 4 shells for final plating. Add saffron; reduce clam broth till one-third. Add cream and reduce to proper consistency, season with salt and pepper and set aside. Peel and dice potatoes, blanch for five minutes. Trim broccoli rabe and blanch for three to four minutes; chill then drain dry. Dice chorizo, slice garlic. Sauté chorizo and garlic to release oils. Add potatoes then broccoli rabe and season.

Sauté black bass in hot oil, skin side down, place weight on fish to keep skin flat; add whole butter until golden brown and crisp, flip to finish cooking. Place hash in a ring mold on plate; mirror the plate with sauce. Place bass down; place a dot of basil oil on the plate at about 2:00. Then place 1 clam shell on plate and put 5 clams in it. Split cherry tomato and place in center of the plate. Garnish clams with chervil. Preparation Time: 1 hour. Cooking Time: 20–25 minutes. Serves 4.

Courtesy of Jim Filip, owner of Doris and Ed's.

Bounty from the Sea

Today, traditional seafood restaurants with nautical décor continue to offer delicious, quality standbys such as clam chowder, stuffed flounder and mixed seafood platters. There are also new kids on the block, trendy bistros and those that serve gourmet seafood. Sushi has become popular, and some shore eateries offer a fusion of both old and new methods of preparing seafood. Oysters as "street food" have had a revival in recent years, with popular outdoor oyster festivals at shore towns including Asbury Park and Red Bank. Seafood festivals at Belmar and other resorts are popular annual events. Long live the joys of biting into a crunchy soft-shell crab, slurping oysters, munching fried clams or ordering the fresh catch of the day.

Down on the Farm

THE GARDEN STATE

New Jersey's nickname, the Garden State, the unfounded target of bad jokes, is usually attributed to the 1876 Philadelphia Centennial Exposition. The exact origin remains debatable, but credit usually goes to the Honorable Abraham Browning of Camden, a former New Jersey attorney general, for using the phrase during a speech he gave at the exposition on New Jersey Day, August 24. In his 1926 two-volume book, *Wagon Jaunts*, author Alfred Heston wrote that Browning compared the state to "an immense barrel filled with good things to eat and open at both ends, with Pennsylvanians grabbing from one end and New Yorkers from the other." (It should be noted that Benjamin Franklin is credited with comparing New Jersey's geographic location to a barrel tapped at both ends way before Browning made his speech.) The huge Philadelphia fair had pavilions from various states that showed off their products, and New Jersey's produce displays were impressive.

Although many farms have gradually been replaced by highways, housing, industrial parks and malls, New Jersey still produces an abundance of fruits and vegetables. The state retains its traditional moniker as the Garden State. There have been changes over the years, as the coastal area that was sustainable in the nineteenth century has lost many of its farms.

In the first half of the twentieth century, before the opening of the Garden State Parkway in the mid-1950s, many old-timers remember riding "down the shore" on highways such as Route 9 and Route 35. They recall stopping along the way at farmers' stands to buy fresh berries, as well as other local fruits and vegetables. It was part of the experience of a seashore vacation or day trip. Today, though farmers' stands still exist on some back roads at the shore, they are not so prevalent on highways. However, farmers' markets and festivals that celebrate fresh produce are gaining in popularity today.

TREASURES OF THE PINELANDS

Though not what most people may think of as the Jersey Shore, the vast area of the New Jersey Pine Barrens is linked with the coastal area. Its pine forests, a still untamed focus of legends, are known for wild foods and natural remedies. In colonial times, the area was a center of bog iron production, but agriculture and tourism are the main industries today. Its sandy, acidic soil didn't prove to be good for settlers to grow traditional crops, but the area supports distinctive forms of plant life. Gathering and foraging continue for some residents who carry on these pursuits as their ancestors did.

Despite its proximity to the Garden State Parkway and boardwalks, the enigmatic region remains mostly rural. Who hasn't heard of the Jersey Devil, the horned and winged creature supposedly born to Mrs. Leeds in 1735 at Leeds Point? The Pine Barrens also has its own style of cooking, including such memorable dishes as chicken foot soup and wild rabbit pie.[21] Home remedies and natural cures are made from Pinelands vegetation. In the mid-nineteenth century, Dr. James Still, known as the "Black Doctor of the Pines," treated many satisfied patients. The son of a former slave, he did not have a traditional medical degree but was knowledgeable and used medicines derived from local plants.

BOUNCING RED BALLS

One of the best-known legendary characters associated with the history of New Jersey agriculture is John "Peg Leg" Webb, who went from seaman to schoolteacher to farmer. In about 1840, Webb started a cranberry bog in Ocean County, New Jersey, near Cassville. He reportedly received as much as fifty dollars per barrel for his cranberries, a hefty sum in those days.

Several versions of a tale about him exist, but they all include Webb having trouble carrying a barrel of cranberries down the steps from his barn loft because of his wooden leg. "Peg Leg" either tripped or decided to dump the berries down the stairs. The good ones bounced all the way down, and the bad ones stayed on the steps. This accidental discovery allegedly led to the practice of cranberry sorters testing to determine which cranberries bounce to separate the superior from the inferior ones. Modern methods of sorting are based on the "bouncing" principle.

Long before Europeans arrived, Native Americans knew the value of cranberries. The luscious red berry, a symbol of peace, was used to make pemmican (a dried preserved meat product), to dye clothing and blankets and to extract poison from wounds, as well as other practical uses. The word "cranberry," first used in America, is derived from a European word meaning "crane" berry. It referred to the cranberry plant's pale pink flower, said to resemble the head of a crane. The Pilgrims were the first New World settlers associated with eating cranberries. Colonists found the cranberry to be too tart for their taste buds. Although the Native Americans did sometimes sweeten them, it was the settlers who felt they needed to add sugar. Over the years, sugar dominated the cranberry delicacies, but today there are recipes using less sugar or alternative sweeteners.

A *Harper's Weekly* article from November 10, 1877, about a shore-area cranberry bog glorified the importance of cranberries with Thanksgiving dinner in the embellished writing of the era:

> *Thanksgiving turkey without cranberries is what life is without matrimony or matrimony without quarrels. The small red spheres of the fruit, crushed, sweetened, and transmuted into a delicious crystalline jelly, bring out all that is so good in the bird's flavor and supplement it so agreeably that no reasonable housekeeper ever thinks of serving it without that sauce, which in its ruddiness of color seems to have caught the very exhilaration of autumn and in its taste combines the sweets and sours to perfection.*

Seasonal cranberry pickers near the coastal town of Tuckerton, Ocean County. *From Harper's Weekly, November 10, 1877.*

The article describes a bog of about 110 acres near West Creek, "an old fishing village on the Tuckerton branch of the New Jersey Southern Railway." The writer visited the bog in late August, when the berries were budding, before they ripened about a month later. He related how the grower became ecstatic as he showed off his berries, with their "exquisite colors, the redness of ripeness not having appeared, and faint blushes of crimson melting into delicate pinks and a bluish creaminess or a soft purple."

Although the berries were undeniably beautiful, the pickers' working conditions are another story. They came from neighboring farms and villages and worked for about five weeks beginning in late summer or early fall. People of all ages gathered the cranberries and were paid about forty cents per bushel. Fishermen who needed to supplement their income were recruited. Women and their young children also toiled in the bogs. Child labor laws were almost nonexistent, and it was commonplace for these children to be kept out of school to work. Although the *Harper's* writer described the picking as festive, the physical demands of long hours bent over in the hot sun were surely not the pleasant pastime as described in some nineteenth-century publications.

CRANBERRY PRODUCTS

In New Egypt, Elizabeth Lee and her brother, Enoch Bills, were the owners of extensive cranberry bogs in the early twentieth century. Supposedly, Elizabeth did not want to waste some damaged berries, so she tried boiling them with sugar and made cranberry sauce that she decided to can. Her sauce was the first canned cranberry sauce and was so popular that her family built a canning factory. They called their product Bog Sweet Cranberry Sauce, and it became a part of Ocean Spray.

Most of the Garden State's cranberries are marketed by Ocean Spray Cranberries Inc., a national growers' cooperative. The Ocean Spray brand began in Massachusetts in 1912, but the Ocean Spray cooperative was created in 1930 by three cranberry growers who wanted to increase the market for their crops. Grower Marcus L. Urann led the group, along with Elizabeth Lee and John Makepeace. Their efforts paid off well. The founders developed new products, such as Ocean Spray Cranberry

Workers are dry harvesting cranberries in the Pinelands, 1920s or 1930s. The wooden scoops designed to protect the delicate berries were eventually replaced with modern machines. *Courtesy of Whitesbog Preservation Trust.*

Juice Cocktail, during their first year in 1930. Over a period of time, they revolutionized the market by adding numerous groundbreaking products using cranberries.

In a promotional 1953 Eatmor recipe booklet, a cartoon housewife looks happy because she can make cranberry sauce in a jiffy. During this decade, "quick and easy" ways to do things were desirable.

10-Minute Cranberry Sauce

2 cups sugar
2 cups water
4 cups Eatmor Cranberrries (one bag or box) [brand is no longer in existence; substitute any kind of fresh New Jersey cranberries]

Boil sugar and water together 5 minutes. Add cranberries and boil without stirring, until all the skins pop open—about 5 minutes. Remove from heat and cool in saucepan. Makes one quart.

VARIATIONS
Cranberry-Ambrosia—Pour sauce over thin-sliced oranges, top with shredded coconut.
Minted Cranberry Sauce—Stir in teaspoon chopped fresh mint or few drops mint extract.
Cranberry Apricot Delight—Add 1 cup cooked sweetened apricots.
Cranberry-Chiquita—Fold in 3 bananas cut in ½-inch slices.
Cranberry-Ruby Pears—Spoon sauce over cooked or canned pear halves.

The production of cranberries continues to be a major industry in New Jersey, especially in Burlington County. The counties at the shore are still producers, but cranberry farms have diminished in coastal areas that have experienced rapid development. Today, the Garden State is the third-biggest cranberry producer in the United States after Wisconsin and Massachusetts.

BLUE BEAUTIES

It wasn't until 2004 that the highbush blueberry (*Vaccinium corymbosum*), a species native to North America, was declared New Jersey's official state fruit. Elementary school children inspired the designation at that time, but the story of its development goes back to the 1910s. Blueberries were first cultivated for commercial production at Whitesbog in Burlington County, about twenty miles inland. Most blueberry farms today are in Hammonton, Atlantic County, about midway between the coast and Philadelphia. The blueberry is a popular fruit at the Jersey Shore. Many seashore hotels and restaurants feature dishes with blueberries, and they are a healthy choice for residents and visitors alike. The story of the first cultivated blueberries is a fascinating one.

The First Lady of Blueberries

Born in the Pine Barrens town of New Lisbon in 1871, Elizabeth Coleman White loved the land from which she came. As a child, she had fun gathering the edible plants and berries of the vast scrubby pine forests. There were pioneers of cranberry farming on both sides of Elizabeth's family. The cranberry bogs developed by her maternal grandfather, James A. Fenwick, formed the basis of the farm that would later be known as Whitesbog.

Before the Civil War, Elizabeth's grandfather, Barclay White, and his five sons picked wild cranberries in the backwoods of the Pinelands. Barclay White was an innovative farmer who served as the superintendent of Indian affairs during President Ulysses S. Grant's administration. One of his sons was Elizabeth's father, Joseph J. White, an engineer who married James A. Fenwick's daughter, Mary, in 1869.

The eldest of four sisters, Elizabeth attended a Quaker school in Philadelphia. She lived with her family at Fenwick Manor in New Lisbon for many years. The feisty Elizabeth achieved financial security and fame by cultivating swamp huckleberries into blueberries. In her early years, she was involved with the family cranberry business. She distinguished herself as the first woman to be a member of the American Cranberry Association, and eventually she would serve as its president.

In December 1910, Elizabeth read about experiments that the U.S. Department of Agriculture was conducting with blueberries, which were still undomesticated at that time. USDA botanist Frederick Coville determined in

Elizabeth Coleman White and Frederick Coville are checking on their blueberries at Whitesbog in 1920. Ms. White was the first to cultivate the blueberry, aided by Coville's scientific knowledge. *Courtesy of Whitesbog Preservation Trust.*

1910 that blueberry plants must be grown in acidic, moist soil, and he soon developed successful ways to improve berry size and flavor. His revelations that blueberries need very low-pH soil, contrary to most plants, led him to publish his work on how to propagate blueberries. Coville is credited as the first to "tame" the blueberry, and his findings were crucial to producing the fruits on a large scale. In 1911, he successfully crossed two wild blueberries, leading to the release of successful hybrids.

Excited about Coville's findings, Elizabeth offered to help him with his experiments. White and Coville made an agreement, and he conducted his research at Whitesbog. Besides providing financial support, Elizabeth drove her horse and buggy around the dirt roads of the pine forest looking for outstanding blueberry plants. She recruited locals to search remote areas to find and tag desirable blueberry bushes that would make good "parents" for new plants. Then Coville would use them in experiments. "Miss Lizzie" reportedly had great respect for her helpers, who were known by the then derogatory term "Pineys." She openly called herself a "Piney" with pride. She even named some varieties of the plants after her workers. In the summer of 1911, she wrote of how Zeke Sooy found three bushes for her. One of them, later known as "the Sooy," had berries as large as ⅝ an inch in diameter.

White and Coville made a good team. He conducted the scientific research while she managed the business of gathering. Just over five years after their alliance began, blueberries were on their way to becoming a huge industry for New Jersey. Starting in 1917, J.J. White Inc. sold berries under the name of Whitesbog Blueberries. In 1923, Elizabeth used her mother's legacy to help fund the building of Suningive, her beloved home in Whitesbog Village, next to her grandfather's cranberry bog.

In 1927, Elizabeth was one of the founders of the New Jersey Blueberry Cooperative Association. Tru-Blu-Berries was the original name of their product, and the boxes were simply wrapped in brown paper. The first woman to receive the New Jersey Department of Agriculture citation, Elizabeth was honored with numerous awards. Besides her role in developing blueberries, Elizabeth White took a deep interest in social welfare and education.

Pioneer food columnist Clementine Paddleford interviewed Elizabeth White in the 1940s. She dubbed her "America's Blueberry Queen" and asked for the lady's favorite recipes. Elizabeth's response was that she thought the best way of all to eat blueberries was not to heat them but rather to enjoy them naturally, perhaps "with a little cream and a dusting of sugar." However, she graciously gave Ms. Paddleford a few recipes that she used when she did cook with her berries.

Blueberry Meringue Pie
(from the kitchen of Elizabeth Coleman White)

3 cups blueberries	1 tablespoon lemon juice
1 cup sugar	2 eggs separated
2 tablespoons flour	1 baked 9-inch pastry shell
¼ teaspoon salt	2 tablespoons powdered sugar

Mix together blueberries, granulated sugar, flour, salt, lemon juice and egg yolks, and cook over boiling water 10 minutes, or until thick, stirring constantly. Cool slightly, turn into baked pastry shell. Cover with meringue made by gradually beating powdered sugar into stiffly beaten egg whites. Bake in moderate oven (350 degrees) about 15 minutes, or until delicately browned.[22] Approximate yield: 1-crust (9-inch) pie.

Courtesy of Whitesbog Preservation Trust.

Now recognized in the annals of women's history, Elizabeth Coleman White lived to see the success of the blueberry industry for the state's growers. She died at Suningive in 1954. Historic Whitesbog is preserved today under the auspices of the Whitesbog Preservation Trust, and the best way to understand its history is to visit and experience the site.

Other delicious berries are also associated with the New Jersey Shore. Numerous strawberry festivals held in the late spring attest to the popularity of that fruit, especially in the Cape May area. Also, blackberries, raspberries, whortleberries and chokeberries grow well along most of the coastal area.

THE EXQUISITE FRUIT OF THE DUNES

One of the wildest and most stunningly beautiful native fruits that grow in sandy soil from Maine to Virginia is the *Prunus maritima*, commonly known as the beach plum. In 1524, explorer Giovanni da Verrazzano called their bushes "damson trees" (a species of plum tree) when he observed them along the coast of southern New York State. Sailing on the *Half Moon* for the Dutch in search of a passage to Asia, Henry Hudson noted many "blue plums" on the banks of what is now the Hudson River in 1609. That same year, Hudson navigated along the Jersey coast, where the beach plums were also abundant. Native Americans and colonists made use of several species of the tart cherry-sized fruits.

"Today, jelly production from wild fruit persists as a cultural tradition in coastal communities throughout the species' range, with hotspots on Cape Cod, eastern Long Island, and at the New Jersey Shore's Island Beach State Park and Cape May. It is also used for dune stabilization and other conservation programs."[23] Attempts have been made for more than a century to bring wild beach plums into cultivation, but none has totally succeeded. Unlike cranberries and blueberries, most beach plums remain undomesticated, giving them an aura of excitement for both scientific and culinary experimenters. They are sturdy plants that resist wind and storms, and yet they are diminishing.

Although beach plums and food products made from them—such as jams, jellies, brandies and baked goods—are often associated with Cape Cod, there's an increasing appreciation of the beach plum in New Jersey.

The Cape May County Beach Plum Association, a nonprofit organization established in 2005, educates the public about beach plums, promotes them as delicious and healthful fruits and stresses their importance to dune restoration. In July 2011, the beach plum was declared the "Official Fruit of Cape May County." Environmental and student groups have been instrumental in helping with government experiments using beach plum seedlings to reestablish the dunes at the Jersey Shore.

Today, in this food-centric age of creative recipes, beach plums are being used in new ways for things such as wine served as an aperitif, a less sugary palate-cleansing sorbet and in vinaigrette salad dressing made with beach plum jam.[24] The beach plum is viewed as a "heritage" crop that comes from a unique background. Progress is being made in the development of a sustainable beach plum industry, but there's still something about the beach plum's spirited unruliness that makes it appealing.

A FORBIDDEN FRUIT

The tomato loves New Jersey soil. Originally from South America, tomatoes were distributed by the Spanish, who colonized parts of America and took seeds back to Europe. Technically it's a fruit, but the tomato is for all practical purposes considered to be a vegetable in the culinary world. Indeed, it is hard to think of eating a tomato for dessert, but myriad recipes for appetizers, main dishes, salads, soups and sauces come to mind.

The tomato belongs to the deadly nightshade family and has an intriguing past, as it was once thought to be a highly poisonous fruit. Tomatoes were known by the French as aphrodisiacs—"pommes d'amour" or "love apples," a name that many Americans readily adopted.

Because of the highly acidic quality of the tomato, it is an excellent choice for canning and became the most popular canned food by the beginning of the twentieth century. In 1869, Joseph Campbell began a canning business in the Garden State that would become the world-famous Campbell's Soup Company. By the 1960s, the tomato canning industry in New Jersey had diminished. Campbell's stopped making soup at Camden in 1980 and discontinued manufacturing there by 1990. Its plant is now in California, but the company maintains its world headquarters in Camden.

Please Pass the Ketchup

Although much of the tomato growing and processing was closer to the urban areas, tomatoes have played a significant role in the food history of the New Jersey Shore. Tomatoes thrive on small farms near the coast, and many Italian restaurants and pizzerias at the seashore resorts have traditionally used locally grown produce. Ketchup is a tomato product that was relevant to the economy at the Jersey Shore and, ultimately, to the world. Ketchup most likely originated in Southeast Asia around the end of the seventeenth century but has gone through many changes since that time. Of course, ketchup today is usually associated with fast foods like burgers and fries, but on Victorian menus, it was one of the numerous condiments offered at the classiest restaurants and hotels.

With an abundance of luscious tomatoes growing in the coastal region of New Jersey, it made sense to can and manufacture tomato products close to their source. Businessman Edward Clarke Hazard recognized an opportunity to capitalize on a growing industry, "fancy groceries," and ketchup became his best-known product.

Born on April 4, 1831, in Rhode Island, E.C. Hazard began his career by selling B.T. Babbets BEST SOAP in 1849 from a horse-drawn wagon in New York City. He eventually owned downtown Manhattan warehouses for wholesale distribution of food products. In 1883, Hazard decided to purchase a 165-acre tract in Shrewsbury, New Jersey, on the north side of Sycamore Avenue, where he operated a state-of-the-art factory, offices and a well-equipped laboratory. Most of the fruits and vegetables to be canned or bottled were grown on nearby farms, and many locals (including women) were employed at the factory.

When Hazard bought the Shrewsbury plant, it was already the site of James Broadmeadow's tomato canning business, but the existing building burned down in 1888. Hazard built a larger facility with major improvements. He soon purchased the 112-acre Loggy Hole Farm on the south side of Sycamore Avenue from James Hance Patterson, and he was able to maintain control over the quality of the produce that he used. E.C. Hazard and Company thrived as one of the largest manufacturers, importers and distributors of fancy food products, with the factory in Shrewsbury and offices at the Mercantile Exchange Building and a "depot" (warehouse) in lower Manhattan. (Both are now luxury condominiums in Tribeca.)

Hazard's Shrewsbury brand included canned tomatoes, asparagus, peppers, mushrooms, burnt onion sauce and jellies. He was an early distributor of

Down on the Farm

A detail from an E.C. Hazard Company letterhead illustrates the Shrewsbury factory in Monmouth County where Hazard's famous "Tomatoketchup" was manufactured.

Tabasco sauce and dozens of household products, but ketchup is the item most people associate with him today. He patented his product as "Tomatoketchup." It is significant that Hazard paid attention to quality and purity during a time when such things were often ignored. Though he wasn't the first or only person to make tomato ketchup (Henry J. Heinz and others were already making ketchup), the conscientious entrepreneur's products were free from additives and labeled "PURE." He even used vats lined with silver to ensure less corrosion and better quality. E.C. Hazard was the founder and longtime president of the Pure Food Manufacturers Association and was influential in establishing the Pure Food and Drug Act of 1906.

An 1890s ad for Shrewsbury Tomatoketchup describes how the product was used: "It is admirable with hot and cold meats, oyster stews, fish, and gives a superior flavor to gravies, deviled kidneys, or any delicate preparation of meat. With chops, veal cutlets and baked beans it is simply delicious and it is a great addition to macaroni or hot buttered toast."

Hazard's family history could easily fill a book. He was married three times and had two sons with his second wife, who died in 1880 at the age of

89

forty-two. He and his third wife, Florence, had eight children. Shrewsbury Manor, a sprawling mansion on Sycamore Avenue with seven towers, forty bedrooms and a grand ballroom, became the family's home. Their son Elmer was a doctor in Long Branch and founded Hazard Hospital; a daughter married an Austrian prince, Francis von Auersperg; and another daughter married Alfred N. Beadleston Sr. (his son was Senator Beadleston), who was sixty when she was twenty-one.

E.C. Hazard died in 1905. His company went bankrupt during the credit panic of 1907, but it was his widow Florence's attempts to gain control over her sons' interests that led to the downfall of the business. In 1911, Hazard's daughter Elizabeth and her husband, Harry Lord Powers, purchased Shrewsbury Manor, the factory and the original recipes. The new venture was called Shrewsbury Manufacturing Company. After a fire razed the factory in 1914, a new, smaller structure was built, but it was also destroyed by fire in 1935 and Hazard's closed permanently. Shrewsbury Manor was torn down in 1937.

An impressive headstone designed by Daniel Chester French memorializes Edward Clarke Hazard at the Christ Church Cemetery at Shrewsbury's historic Four Corners. Perhaps E.C. Hazard's greatest legacy is his insistence on unadulterated canned and bottled foods. He was truly a Victorian entrepreneur with foresight who took pride in the quality of his products.

FRUITS OF SUCCESS

In the nineteenth and early twentieth centuries, an abundance of orchards prospered, not only inland but also within a few miles of the Jersey coastline. Apples and peaches were plentiful, but in areas in eastern Monmouth County such as Middletown and Hazlet, suburban development of houses, condominiums and shopping centers has taken over most of them. Though houses have also mushroomed in Western Monmouth County, there are still some commercial orchards there.

The delightful aroma of juicy Jersey peaches fills the kitchen while the following flavorsome cake is baking. It's perfect for dessert or with afternoon tea. This recipe could be described as a "peach upside down cake."

Fresh Peach Cake

¼ cup butter
3½ cups fresh peaches
1 cup sugar
1 tsp. vanilla
½ tsp. salt

½ cup brown sugar
3 eggs
½ cup milk
1 teaspoon baking powder
1½ cups flour

Melt butter in 8-in. square baking pan over low flame. Remove from stove, sprinkle with brown sugar. Place peach halves, cut side down, in the butter and brown sugar, arranging them in 3 rows each way on bottom of pan. This uses 9 peach halves and will make 9 square servings. Beat egg yolks until light and lemon colored; blend in sugar and continue beating until smooth. Blend in milk and vanilla. Sift dry ingredients and fold into first mixture. Fold in stiffly beaten egg whites. Pour the batter over the peaches in the baking pan. Bake at 350 degrees for 50–60 minutes (or until a knife inserted in center comes out clean). Serve warm with whipped cream.

From Mrs. J.W. Goodliffe Jr.'s New Jersey's Own Cook Book, *Women's Association of the Elmora Presbyterian Church, Elizabeth, New Jersey, 1949. Special Collections and University Archives, Rutgers University Libraries.*

THOUSANDS OF PIES

Delicious Orchards on Route 34 in Colt's Neck is often a stop for shore visitors and is popular with locals as well. It was opened in 1911 and was managed by three generations of the Barclay family. After World War II, Carroll W. Barclay changed the business from completely wholesale to a partial mix with retail. In 1959, Barclay set up a makeshift apple stand that was a big success, and by the following year, he had constructed a 1,200-square-foot stand with a big variety of apples, which were all hand-picked. He added apple cider and his wife Janet's apple pies (her recipe is still used today).

In the 1960s, the Barclays' business became year round. Janet, with a crew of local helpers, was baking more than three thousand pies per week. In 1966, the Barclays bought a red brick building to use as an indoor store on Route 34 where Delicious Orchards remains today. The Barclays kept expanding and brought in Carroll's sister, Carolyn, and her husband, Bill Smith. They added products such as cookies, donuts and cakes, as well as a variety of grocery items, to complement their fresh produce. They made up attractive gift baskets and established a mail-order business. The Barclays and Smiths sold Delicious Orchards in 1977 to their management team, Tom Gesualdo, Bill McDonald and Frank McMahon. Today, McDonald and his family are the sole owners, and Delicious Orchards is flourishing and keeping up the traditions and high quality established by the Barclays over a century ago.

THE LITTLE SILVER FARM STAND THAT GREW AND GREW

Today's bustling Sickles Market in Little Silver has a history of growing and selling its produce that goes back to 1908. Harold and Elsie Sickles farmed the land where the market is located on Harrison Avenue, off Rumson Road on acreage acquired from Harold's mother's family, the Parkers. The origins of the historic property can be traced to 1663, when Peter Parker of Rhode Island was awarded a land grant from the king of England.

Ultimately, Harold Sickles's father married a Parker daughter, and their son, Robert Sickles, began to work with his parents in 1945. Previously, the farm sold produce to local stores, but Robert and his wife, Adelaide, opened a seasonal fruit and vegetable stand so they could sell directly to the public. Besides the Harrison Avenue property, Robert "Bob" Sickles also farmed additional land in various parts of Monmouth County, while Adelaide managed the stand with the help of her children. In 1978, at the age of fourteen, Robert "Bob" Sickles Jr. was already involved in buying produce from other local farms to supplement their own crops.

Their popular Little Silver stand kept expanding over the years and today is a unique, up-to-date market. Besides fresh produce, it has gourmet foods, baked goods, flowers, plants, garden supplies and more. It also offers many special events. Bob Sickles Jr. oversees the business, which has an ever-growing number of customers, neighbors from the Jersey Shore and from around the globe.

Down on the Farm

Try these easy-to-make, delectable Sickles family recipes that have been handed down through several generations.

Mrs. Sickles' Fried Green Tomatoes

A southern favorite…made with New Jersey's finest! New Jersey tomatoes are the best in the country…for tenderness, juiciness and flavor!

4 Sickles green tomatoes (firm)
1 egg (beaten)
1 cup Italian breadcrumbs
margarine
salt and pepper

Wash tomatoes, slice ¾-inch pieces. Dip slices into egg and then breadcrumbs. Melt margarine in skillet. Add tomato slices. Cook until golden brown, turning once. Salt and pepper to taste.

Miss Julia Parker's and Mrs. Adelaide Sickles' Apple Crumb

CRUMB
⅓ cup melted butter
1 egg
½ cup sugar

1½ cup flour
1 tsp baking powder
½ tsp salt

Mix with fork. Set aside.

PREP
Slice 5 to 6 apples in 8-in. square pan. Sprinkle with 1 cup of sugar and cinnamon. Cover with crumbs; bake 45 min. (or until apples are done) in oven at 350 degrees. Serve with whipped cream.

Recipes courtesy of Sickles Market, Little Silver.

The Parker homestead and farm dates back to the late seventeenth century. It was once known as the Parker Sickles Farm. Julia Parker was born at the site in 1899 and still lived there when she died in 1995. She conveyed her family property on Rumson Road to the Borough of Little Silver to be preserved as a park and museum, and it was recently added to the New Jersey Register of Historic Places and the National Register of Historic Places.

ANIMAL HUSBANDRY

In the nineteenth century, there were numerous dairies along the Jersey coast and cattle farms that raised animals for meat. Pigs, hogs and sheep were prevalent, and the shore area had plenty of meat, dairy and produce available locally, as well as grain from other areas of New Jersey. But as meat products became more readily obtainable from the Midwest and West with improvements in transportation and refrigeration, the animal farms dwindled, and there were few left by the mid-twentieth century. Only a small number of coastal dairy farms remain in business today.

Cattle once grazed in tranquil meadows along the boggy coastline, as illustrated in the Woolman and Rose atlas of 1878 that depicts the Cranmoor Farm in Toms River. The farm belonged to John P. Haines, who had a reputation for being good to his animals. In the first half of the twentieth century, Cranmoor Farm became a country club, and some of the land was developed for housing. In Monmouth County, cows were seen grazing in the marshlands of Belmar and Little Silver, among other areas that are now developed, and it's hard to imagine that there were pastures where houses now stand.

COUNT YOUR CHICKENS AND YOUR EGGS

Commercial poultry farms were once widespread at the Jersey Shore. It was also common for restaurants and hotels (as well as individuals) to raise their own chickens, ensuring a supply of fresh eggs and meat. This practice is becoming more common again today with an increased interest in sustainable living.

Down on the Farm

At the Eigenrauch's Middletown farm, Alfred deWinter, Henry Eigenrauch Sr. and Dr. Justus H. Eigenrauch Sr. (left to right) prepare to butcher a white leghorn hen in 1919. *Courtesy of Jane Eigenrauch.*

In 1915, poultryman Henry Eigenrauch Sr. of Middletown shows one of his white leghorns to Herbert W. Eigenrauch, the second oldest of his four sons. *Courtesy of Jane Eigenrauch.*

Eigenrauch Farms was founded in 1911 when Henry and Jessie Eigenrauch of Jersey City purchased a sixty-six-acre produce farm on Chapel Hill Road in Middletown. When the two hundred chickens that Jessie began raising became a profitable egg-producing flock, Eigenrauch Farms soon developed into a successful egg farm and hatchery, selling eggs wholesale to local groceries, restaurants and bakeries and shipping baby chicks to poultry farms throughout the mid-Atlantic states until 1933. Robert Eigenrauch, Henry and Jessie's third of four sons, rebuilt the wholesale egg portion of the business in 1936 and ran it for fifty years. During this period, Eigenrauch Farms purchased and processed eggs first from local farmers and later from farms in Georgia, Minnesota and Pennsylvania and distributed them throughout central New Jersey and along the Jersey Shore. In 1985, Robert sold the business to a Pennsylvania company.

Jessie Eigenrauch's Butterscotch Pudding

Jessie's four young sons enjoyed this pudding, which their mother made with fresh eggs from their Middletown farm and milk from the family's cow.

2 cups brown sugar
4 tablespoons butter
4 tablespoons flour
2 teaspoons corn starch
2 teaspoons vanilla
2 cups milk
4 eggs
¼ teaspoon salt

Mix dry ingredients. Add milk. Heat until thickened. Add some of the thickened mixture to beaten eggs. Combine and heat a few minutes more. Add butter and vanilla. Cool. Eat as pudding; for a pie, pour into baked pie shell. Top with whipped cream.

Courtesy of Jane Eigenrauch.

Down on the Farm

During the 1920s and 1930s, a number of Jewish people who were being persecuted in Europe relocated to New York in search of a better life. Some of these emigrés were encouraged by the Jewish Agricultural Society to begin poultry farming in New Jersey. They started farms in Howell, Farmingdale, Freehold and Jackson. The Jewish poultry industry was very successful, and at its peak in the 1930s, Monmouth County was considered the leading egg producer in the United States. However, the rapid development and building of housing in the 1950s and 1960s, as well as economic change, contributed to the decline of the poultry farms.[25]

Nevertheless, there are some poultry farms along the coast today, even with fresh turkeys to go with the Jersey cranberry sauce. Hinck's Turkey Farm, established in 1938 by Richard Hinck, is run by the same family today. Their sprawling farm is located in Wall Township, where their free-range turkeys have plenty of room. In the mid-1950s, the Hinck's store was housed in a former diner in Neptune, but today the company operates a modern retail facility in Manasquan that sells a variety of turkey products and does catering.

Buy Local

Besides tomatoes and corn, an abundance of produce—including lima beans, green beans, bell peppers, sweet corn, asparagus, squash, eggplant, potatoes, peas, string beans, beets, spinach, cucumbers, melons and more—is still grown on the remaining farmland of the New Jersey coastal region.

It's always an exciting time when the sweet Jersey corn is ready to eat. It goes with almost any meal, but it is especially fun to eat corn on the cob served with soft-shell crabs or steamed clams. Young, tender ears of sweet corn are called "green" corn. Following is another way that fresh Jersey corn on the cob was used about a century ago. Notice the phrase "as large as a hen's egg," a clear but outmoded way to measure.

In this circa 1920 photo, a variety of produce from communities in Cape May County is arranged for display, probably at a fair. (The Pomona Grange is the categorical name for the county divisions of the National Grange.) *Courtesy of Judy and Larry Wietsma.*

Green Corn Soup

"One dozen ears of corn to 1 gallon of water; boil the cobs 1 hour after grating off the corn. After skimming, put in the corn and boil 1 hour. Put in large onion cut fine and fried light brown in piece of butter and lard, each as large as a hen's egg; also 5 tomatoes cut fine and season[ed]. Fifteen minutes before taking off, stir in one cup milk, 1 tablespoon flour; strain." *From* The Ladies Aid Cook Book, *First Baptist Church, Keyport, early 1900s. Special Collections and University Archives, Rutgers University Libraries.*

Farm to Table

The idea of growing one's food in the backyard or buying it from a local farm, farmers' market or CSA (Community Supported Agriculture) and bringing it fresh to the table is, of course, not a new one. In essence, it surely goes back to whenever man first sat down at a table to eat.

During the world wars, Americans realized the economic importance of rationing and growing their own foods in their backyards. Victory gardens were encouraged during the Second World War, and indeed most everyone who had a backyard grew at least some of their own produce. Along the Jersey coast, such gardens were plentiful, and food businesses often operated their own farms. "Farm to table," when used by restaurants, usually implies that the food on the table came from a specific farm. There are an increasing number of restaurants at the Jersey Shore and throughout the state that have their own farms.

In Cape May, the Ebbitt Room is a stylish restaurant in the charming Virginia Hotel. The establishment utilizes a special sixty-acre tract called Beach Plum Farm in West Cape May only a few miles from the restaurant. The farm inspires seasonal specialties for the gourmet dishes that are served. During the twentieth century, the tract was used as grazing land for a dairy farm and for growing lima beans and soybeans. But in 2007, when Curtis Bashaw, co-managing partner in Cape Resorts Group (CRG), purchased the farm, the land was uncultivated and overgrown with weeds. Bashaw recognized the opportunity that the tract would provide to grow produce and raise livestock for CRG's restaurants (the Ebbitt Room, the Blue Pig Tavern and the Rusty Nail). His paternal grandfather had a small "weekend" farm in the Cherry Hill area. His maternal grandmother, who ran the old Christian Admiral Hotel in Cape May, used a farm in Port Norris to grow berries and other crops for her hotel in the 1960s and 1970s.

Bashaw's background gave him added incentive for the project, and he successfully restored Beach Plum Farm, which now yields asparagus and berries—strawberries, blackberries and raspberries—as well as sweet potatoes, tomatoes and even the mint leaves for cocktails and the flowers on the tables. Farm-fresh eggs are a recent addition, with chicken coops now in place. Everything is useful; the chicken waste is used for fertilizer, and the pigs consume leftovers from the restaurants.[26]

For this type of "farm to table" operation, the practice of growing food close to where it will be consumed is known as "slow food," and there is increasing interest in the slow food movement, which was first organized in

The Hotel Dennis on the Atlantic City Boardwalk (now part of Bally's Resort and Casino) promoted its "farm to table" dining. This circa 1920s or 1930s postcard is of the hotel's local farm.

The elegant main dining room at the Hotel Dennis in Atlantic City as it looked in the 1920s and 1930s. The fresh produce from the hotel's own farm ended up on the dinner tables here.

Italy during the mid-1980s. Also, in the Jersey Shore region, there's more demand in recent years for vegetarian options on menus and vegan selections.

"JERSEY FRESH"

Most Jersey folks have always known how good their local produce is, but as exports shipped from other states and countries became increasingly common, something needed to be done. "Jersey Fresh" was developed by the state as a logo and label to promote New Jersey produce. A voluntary program, "Jersey Fresh" has been embraced by farmers, vendors and consumers as a sign of quality and authenticity that the products are grown in New Jersey. The produce is certified, and farmers must register with the state and pass inspections to meet quality standards before they can display the "Jersey Fresh" seal.

The local produce may cost a little more than imported products, but it is well worth it. When ripe, the crops harvested from the shore region taste great.

The Long Branch Farmers' Market in the 1920s. Many farmers still used horse-drawn wagons, but otherwise the scene is not so different from markets at shore towns today.

Prohibition, the Depression and Beyond

When America went dry, the food and beverage industries suffered a devastating blow. Women's temperance groups finally got their way with the ratification of the Eighteenth Amendment to the Constitution in 1919 that forbade the "manufacture, sale or transportation of intoxicating liquors." National prohibition went into effect on January 17, 1920, and allegedly caused many restaurants to go out of business. Nevertheless, it was relatively easy to find a drink anywhere in the United States during prohibition. As a side effect, the production of soft drinks, candy and ice cream increased. Gourmet cooking took a back seat. Wines used for cooking were allowed on a limited basis, but some were loaded with salt so that they would not be drinkable. Prohibition lasted almost thirteen years, until it was repealed in 1933.

CANDY IS DANDY

Candy and desserts became the legal "addictions" when alcohol was prohibited. Ice cream parlors and stands came up with trendy new names just as bartenders previously concocted drinks with clever names; now there were treats such as the Buster Brown and Turkey Trot ice cream sundaes.[27]

A 1925 rotogravure postcard of Asbury Park shows busy refreshment stands in the middle of the boardwalk and Coca-Cola signs in the background.

Oddly enough, there was even an occurrence of prohibiting candy. A *New York Times* article on July 30, 1923, reported:

> ENDS CANDYLESS SUNDAYS: RESTAURANT MAN GIVES FREE TAFFY
> IN BLUE-LAW TOWN. *Ocean City's fifth candyless Sunday since the enforcement of Lord's Day regulations was ameliorated today by the free distribution of 1,000 boxes of salt water taffy to confectionary-hungry excursionists. John C. Funk, manager of the Arcadia restaurant, staged the candy barbeque. The situation was further relieved when William F. Shriver and J. Frank Shellenberger dispensed ice cream and soda water for the first time on Sunday since the blue ordinance was enforced. Since that time they had kept their places closed on Sunday.*

Ocean City has always been dry, with its Methodist origins going back to the 1870s, so it did seem a bit too much not to allow candy.

At most New Jersey Shore resorts, people had access to both sweet confections and liquor. Candy shops were wildly popular at the boardwalks, while bootlegging and rumrunning along the Jersey coast made alcohol easy to get if you paid the right price. For some restaurateurs and hotel owners, it was business as usual. But alcohol trafficking was a dangerous game, organized by gangsters and corrupt political bosses who exerted fear and influence over the hotel and restaurant owners. All along the Jersey coast, confrontations between the rumrunners and the U.S. Coast Guard ensued. Yet the champagne flowed. Jazz musicians played and flappers danced the Charleston in clubs where illegal booze was served. Prohibition simply didn't work; it was too hard to enforce.

Speak Easy and Eat Well

Speakeasies operated all along the Jersey coast during prohibition. Usually, all you had to do to gain access was to say the proverbial "Joe sent me." Some were in back rooms at restaurants or hotels, but many of them existed in the cellars of private homes. Buyers of old seashore houses, even today, are finding hidden staircases and secret rooms that were once used for drinking illicit booze.

A few resident moose heads kept patrons company on the porch of DeLisle's during the 1920s. Located in a wooded area of Allaire in Monmouth County, it is known to have been a popular speakeasy.

DeLisle's in Allaire Village, a Monmouth County restaurant known to have been a speakeasy, attracted a well-to-do crowd. Famous for its fine French cuisine, the place was a charming country house with a peanut-stone porch. Patrons could dine on the porch or choose the formal indoor dining room.

The customers consumed lots of apple whiskey and then raced around the property in their Model T Fords. In the 1950s, a still was discovered on the third floor of the nearby Allaire Village General Store by state park employees, giving credence to the stories that DeLisle's served bootlegged liquor. The restaurant no longer exists, and the whiskey-making apparatus disappeared from the store.[28]

Another famous restaurant reputed to have served illegal alcohol was Ross Fenton Farm in Wanamassa, just north of Asbury Park. The picturesque "farm" on Deal Lake had both indoor and outdoor dining areas and bungalows for rent. Vaudeville performers Mabel Fenton and Charlie Ross founded the farm in 1899. Small excursion boats would ferry customers over to the restaurant, and locals would hang around in their canoes on the lake, listening to the music of the jazz bands and famous singers who performed there.

Tearooms popped up everywhere in the 1920s, from the Atlantic City Boardwalk to small towns, with most of them actually serving tea. The patrons were not all dowdy ladies; tearooms were actually considered trendy and chic. An unknown number of these establishments were loosely veiled fronts for illegal booze operations. Ross Fenton Farm advertised "afternoon tea."

The Knife and Fork Inn

The Flemish-style design of Atlantic City's Knife and Fork Inn is said to have been inspired by a storybook illustration, but the historic landmark's illustrious past is far from being a children's tale. It was opened in 1912 as an exclusive gentleman's club for the local bigwigs. Established by William Riddle, the mayor of Atlantic City at that time, and the infamous Louis Kuehnle, known as "the Commodore," the club blatantly served alcohol during prohibition. Women were not allowed at the bar. They were relegated to a "ladies lounge" on the second floor that also had intimate curtained dining alcoves. The third and fourth floors housed private gambling areas and other rooms, the purpose of which can be left to the imagination. The club got away with the illegal booze for a few years, probably thanks to its shrewd associate Enoch "Nucky" Johnson. Nevertheless, federal agents raided the place and seized its supply of liquor.

As a result, the club's membership dropped, and in 1927, it was leased by Milton Latz, a traveling salesman turned restaurateur. He eliminated the bar, thinking that prohibition would never end. During the depression, Latz moved with his wife and kids into the formerly scandalous upstairs rooms. The Knife and Fork survived the famed hurricane of 1944, but the surrounding area was devastated and Latz was able to purchase the restaurant. Milton and his wife, Evelyn, ran the restaurant, but he died in 1948. Their sons, Mack and Jim, took over and operated the restaurant successfully for several decades but were known to have had differences. In 1985, Mack bought out his brother's share and ran the place for a decade, but he was aging and wanted to find a buyer. He couldn't and had to shut down the Knife and Fork in 1997. It was reopened in 1999 when Mack's son, Andrew, leased it. A few years later, Mack resumed his search for a buyer, but the place was in a state of decline.

A woodcut reproduced on a vintage postcard of Atlantic City's famous Knife and Fork Inn at Atlantic and Pacific Avenues is from the 1940s, when it was owned by the Latz family. *Courtesy of Jo Ann Vincent.*

Lobster Thermidor

4 ea. 2.25 lb. lobster
2 tbs. unsalted butter
¼ bunch tarragon
1 ea. minced peeled shallots
6 ea. sliced crimini mushrooms
1 ea. halved lengthwise and sliced leek
2 fl. oz. sherry wine
1 tbs. Dijon mustard
½ cup heavy cream
kosher salt to taste
ground white pepper to taste

LOBSTER PREP
Submerge lobsters in boiling water for 4 minutes. Remove from pot and submerge in an ice water bath. When cool, remove claws and knuckles, then de-shell the meat and cut into large pieces. Split the body of the lobster lengthwise down the center of their backs (be careful not to cut all the way through; you need to use the shell to serve the finished product in), spread body and tail apart. Remove tail meat and cut into the same size pieces as the claw and knuckle meat. Rinse out cavity of the lobster and set aside.

FOR THE SAUCE
Sweat shallots and leeks in butter until slightly translucent. Add tarragon and mushrooms; sweat until wilted and moisture is released. Add lobster meat; sauté for one minute. Add sherry off of flame, flambé, and then stir in Dijon. Add heavy cream; adjust salt and pepper to taste. On a sheet pan, spoon the meat and sauce mixture into the cavity (body and tail) of lobster; remaining sauce can be drizzled on top. Place in 350 degree oven for 10 minutes and then serve.

Courtesy of Executive Chef Michael Newkirk, Knife and Fork Inn.

Fortunately, in 2005, the historic inn was purchased by energetic restaurateur Frank Dougherty, who runs the aforementioned Dock's Oyster House (his family's business since it began in the 1890s). He refurbished the Knife and Fork Inn and transformed it into an outstanding restaurant with the motto "Nucky ate here, shouldn't you?" Dougherty painstakingly preserved the look and feel of the Roaring Twenties while modernizing the kitchen.

A specialty of the Knife and Fork Inn for half a century, and likely served since it began, is the lobster thermidor, a lavish dish with an intriguing past. In 1894, it was allegedly created in Paris to celebrate the opening of *Thermidor*, a play by Victorien Sardou that was showing at a theater near Marie's restaurant in the Boulevard Saint-Denis. Although the French Revolution had taken place one hundred years earlier, it was still a sensitive topic, and the politically charged play was banned after only three performances. "Thermidor" was a summer month on the French Revolutionary calendar during which conspiracies, called the "Thermidorian Reaction," led to the execution of Robespierre and ended the Reign of Terror.

In the old days, live lobsters were split down the middle (perhaps thinking of the guillotine?), but today they are cooked first. The Knife and Fork Inn is one of the few, and probably the only, restaurant in Atlantic City to offer this extravagant and delectable dish.

ATLANTIC CITY'S FABLED SUPPER CLUBS

In the era before casinos, from the 1920s to the early 1960s, Atlantic City was jumping with nightlife. In 1920, an aspiring young singer named Blanche Babbitt left a small town in Pennsylvania for the glamour of Atlantic City. She met Dan Stebbins, who operated the Golden Inn, a small club on Pacific Avenue near Mississippi Avenue. They got married and turned Dan's club into a hot spot for bootlegged liquor and gambling. They renamed it Babette's (Blanche's stage name). She had a knack for designing costumes, arranging music, directing the chorus girls and introducing the acts. The club specialized in charcoal broiled steaks and a variety of seafood. Stars such as Eleanor Powell, Milton Berle and Joe Penner appeared nightly. Visitors included gangster Al Capone and Mayor Jimmy Walker of New York.

A federal investigation in the 1930s targeted Babette's for gambling and illegal horse betting. A raid was conducted in 1943, and bookmaking equipment was seized. Stebbins had to pay thousands of dollars in fines. In 1950, Blanche and Dan Stebbins sold the club. Dan died in 1960, with Blanche passing in 1963. A fictionalized version of Babette's is featured in the first season (2010) of the HBO television series *Boardwalk Empire*. The period costumes and details were meticulously re-created, but the supper club set is based around a Mississippi riverboat bar, different from the real Babette's nautical bar.

Other famous nightclubs in the vicinity of Kentucky Avenue that have become legends include Paul "Skinny" D'Amato's 500 Club, Club Harlem and Grace's Little Belmont. Celebrities associated with the clubs from the 1930s to the 1960s include Frank Sinatra, Dean Martin and Jerry Lewis. These supper clubs served steaks, chops and seafood but were more about drinks, music and other entertainment than food. Today, Atlantic City's nightlife and restaurants with entertainment are located mostly within the big casinos.

WASH'S RESTAURANT

A popular Northside eatery—not a nightclub but on Kentucky Avenue near the clubs—was Wash's Restaurant. It was a tiny place owned by an African American couple who served delicious food. Wash's had several changes of name and location but "has always been maintained by the same family, and is one of the oldest black-owned businesses in the Greater Atlantic City Area."[29] In 1925, the newlyweds moved to Atlantic City from Virginia. After having seven children and making it through the worst of the Great Depression, they opened Wash's Restaurant in 1937. At first, they only had six tables. The establishment grew and became a favorite of the stars who performed at the clubs, including Count Basie, Redd Foxx, Nipsey Russell and Moms Mabley. In the 1950s, Wash's moved to a larger place on Arctic Avenue and became Wash's and Sons Seafood Restaurant, but it suffered during the turbulent 1960s and shut down in the 1970s. The business relocated to Pleasantville, where Wash's Inn, a restaurant and catering service, has remained in the family.[30]

THE RISE OF ETHNIC EATERIES

Besides its notoriety for speakeasies and jazzy supper clubs, the 1920s proved to be a time when individually owned ethnic restaurants gained popularity. A variety of multicultural eateries opened in America during the 1920s and 1930s. The food was good and the prices affordable.

Atlantic City, because of its abundance of tourists and its diverse population, probably had more ethnic eateries than any other place along the Jersey coast. People in the Roaring Twenties were ready to try new foods. Italian, Jewish, Greek and Irish food were already prevalent, but more unusual and exotic cuisines were gaining favor with Americans. Chinese restaurants became widespread, with several opening in Atlantic City and gradually along the coast.

Jewish-owned resort hotels had been featuring kosher food for years. On the Atlantic City Boardwalk, the beautiful Breakers catered to a Jewish clientele. Mrs. Herman Silverman, a summer visitor for much of the first half of the twentieth century, recalled dining there: "They'd give you a beautiful holiday meal…From soup to nuts! With wine, gefilte fish, and soup

Chinese restaurants were becoming widespread by the 1930s and 1940s. The Dragon's Den was located near the Warner Theater on the Atlantic City Boardwalk. Another well-known restaurant, Chinaland, was located on South Tennessee Avenue. *Courtesy of Jo Ann Vincent.*

with knaidlach, roast chicken, knishes, candied sweet potatoes, and all kinds of goodies."[31] The Breakers was imploded in 1974 to make way for casinos.

For more informal Jewish food, Kornblau's at Virginia and Pacific Avenues was famous for its corned beef and hot pastrami sandwiches. In 1946, Lou and Helen Adelman opened Lou's in Ventnor and served classic deli food. And in Asbury Park, at Grossman's Deli on Main Street, Joseph M. Grossman would carve his "world famous corned beef" from a two-hundred-year-old family recipe in the window of his shop for all to see.[32]

After the Second World War, more ethnic eateries opened as soldiers came back from Europe and the Pacific. They wanted foods they had grown accustomed to. Today, a variety of restaurants—Thai, Vietnamese, Mexican, Portuguese, Peruvian and Middle Eastern—is cropping up at the shore.

Despite competition from the big casinos, small historic restaurants can be found in today's Atlantic City. Chef Vola's, established in 1921 by Italian immigrant Pina Vola and later run by cook Ed Gold, is a classic eatery where reservations are a must; it is tucked away in the basement of a private house on South Albion Place. It belongs to the Esposito family, who have owned it since 1982. Some of Vola's sauces made from her recipes using San Marzano tomatoes are still being used (as of 2011), and the Sicilian chicken cacciatore is an original recipe.[33]

The Irish Pub in Atlantic City at St. James Place and the Boardwalk is a historic eatery with guestrooms upstairs that retain the aura of Victorian times. Like many of the other older restaurants, the Irish Pub was a speakeasy during prohibition. Today, at this busy bar and restaurant, customers can have their choice of a thick stout or a creamy lager while listening to toe-tapping Irish music and eating delicious food. Photos of celebrity patrons decorate the walls. The "Yankee Clipper" Joe DiMaggio, who died in 1999, was a regular visitor during the last fifteen years of his life. Since 1972, the Irish Pub has been owned by Dick and Cathy Burke, who have also operated the Irish Pub in Philadelphia since 1980.

Another classic Atlantic City restaurant is Angelo's Fairmount Tavern, 2300 Fairmount Avenue, owned by the Mancuso family. It has been in business since 1935, has expanded its space and is flourishing. The walls are covered with photos, sports memorabilia and pictures of celebrities who have visited the restaurant over the years.

Many of the famous independent Atlantic City restaurants of the twentieth century are gone now. But the names of Shumsky's, The Vienna,

Jack Guishard's, Lou Tendler's Steak House, Mammy's (a doughnut shop on the Boardwalk run by boxer Tendler's wife), The Stanley, Junior's and Sid Hartfield's, the Carolina Grill and others all occupy a place in Atlantic City's diverse culinary history.

Sophisticated Hotel Dining

The Roaring Twenties was a time of contrasts. Although simpler, easy-to-prepare foods were becoming more common, some shore towns also experienced significant revivals of fine dining and classy hotels. The meals would never equal the Victorian menus, but people were celebrating the end of World War I and had money to spend. New hotels cropped up at both large and small resort towns.

Asbury Park's historic brick Berkeley Carteret hotel, opened in 1925, has been reincarnated as the Berkeley Oceanfront Hotel. It is currently home to the Dauphin Grille, serving "seasonal bistro fare." In Red Bank, the beautiful Colonial-style Molly Pitcher Inn on the banks of the Navesink, opened in 1929, has thrived continuously as a hotel and restaurant for fine dining and special events. In Shrewsbury, the lovely Shadowbrook, once a private home, has been a favorite restaurant and banquet venue since the 1940s. As a refined resort in Spring Lake that was known for its well-to-do Irish summer residents, the Essex and Sussex provided superior oceanfront accommodations and food to visitors for decades. It still stands but is now a condominium.

Atlantic City experienced a building boom with many big hotels opening, including the Ritz Carlton in 1921, where the infamous "Nucky" Johnson maintained his quarters. It is a condominium today. The Claridge, the last bastion of the big pre-casino hotels to be built, was opened in 1930 and has remained open ever since. It's now one of the popular hotel-casinos. The Atlantic City skyline of the 1920s provided a spectacular panorama of huge hotels, and they all had dining rooms. Today's hotel-casinos carry on the tradition of fine dining but also offer buffets, casual restaurants, bars and fast-food options.

The Flanders hotel in the dry town of Ocean City opened in 1923. The Spanish Mission Revival–style hotel, designed by architect Vivian Smith (who was born in Ocean City), survived the Great Fire of 1927

"The American Plan" dining room of the Flanders, a luxury hotel built in the 1920s at Ocean City, appears busy in this circa 1930s photo.

that destroyed much of the Ocean City Boardwalk. It is still in operation, and Emily's Ocean Room Café at the Flanders is named for the lovely ghost of Emily, an ethereal young woman in white who ostensibly haunts the hotel.

In 1937, Smith also designed the attractive building that became the Chatterbox restaurant on East Ninth Street. It's in business today. Here legendary screen star Grace Kelly, later the princess of Monaco, reportedly worked as a waitress. Her well-known family from Philadelphia summered in Ocean City for many years.

THIRST QUENCHERS

Lemonade, root beer and colas were among the favorite beverages sold at boardwalks, piers and soda fountains at the shore. New drinks were soon developed in lieu of alcohol. The soft drink Yoo-hoo began

In 1923, an unidentified girl sells lemon juice and Hires root beer at a stand near the entrance to the old Long Branch Pier (in the area that is today's Pier Village).

in New Jersey during the 1920s when an Italian-American family named Oliveri was making Tru-Fruit drinks; Natale Oliveri decided to add a chocolate beverage to their repertoire. But it was the trendy beverage called Bevo that was the big winner at refreshment stands on the Atlantic City Boardwalk. It was a nonalcoholic malt drink, a type of "near beer" with a very low alcohol content, less than 0.5 percent alcohol by volume, the standard legally accepted for non-alcohol products according to the Volstead Act. Bevo was manufactured by St. Louis brewery Anheuser-Busch.

How to make Prohibition-Era Lemonade

"Lemonade is entitled to the first place on the list of fruit beverages, refreshing as it is in itself, and capable as it is of numerous variations. Proportions for mixing are 3 times as much sugar as lemon juice, and 6 times as much water, but it may be wise to hold back part of the sugar until after mixing, in case it should be too sweet. It is quite easy to add more sugar, but not so easy to add more lemon juice and water. In hot weather it is most convenient to have lemonade syrup on tap. It will keep in the refrigerator for a week."[34]

During prohibition, some loopholes existed in the system that permitted legal alcohol. Drinks containing alcohol could be prescribed for certain ailments by medical doctors. Wine could be made legally at home, and it was allowed for various religious sacraments. A few manufacturers of wine and spirits found creative ways to circumvent the law that allowed them to remain officially in business. Their goal was to hold out until the end of prohibition, but it was much longer than they had anticipated.

Laird's Applejack ("America's Oldest Native Distillery") in Colt's Neck has a long history that can be traced back to the owners' ancestors who settled in seventeenth-century Monmouth County. Their first recorded commercial sale was in 1780. Applejack, an apple brandy, was extremely popular and profitable throughout the nineteenth century. During prohibition, the Lairds managed to find creative ways to stay in business by manufacturing other apple products such as sweet cider and applesauce. In 1933, the company was granted a license to make and sell medicinal apple brandy. Although it was near the end of prohibition, this gave the company an advantage as it had an inventory ready to sell as soon as it was allowed to. The Jack Rose, a cocktail served today became, popular in the 1920s and 1930s.

Jack Rose

1 oz. lemon juice
½ oz. Grenadine
2 oz. Laird's AppleJack
dash of egg white, if desired

Shake well with ice and strain into a cocktail glass, or serve over ice.

From lairdandcompany.com/recipes_cocktails.htm.

At the height of prohibition, Monmouth County's historic Lincroft Inn developed a reputation for fine food and drink. In 1927, Dante and Mary Daverio purchased the restaurant. According to the Lincroft Inn's website, Mary prepared tasty meals on a coal stove and Dante crafted homemade "spirits" in the cellar. The Daverio family owns the restaurant today, and it's run by Executive Chef/General Manager Denise Wolf. The menu features northern Italian and Continental cuisine. A short distance west of Garden State Parkway's Exit 109, the Lincroft Inn has roots that go back to the late 1600s. The section of the present building where the main bar is located dates to 1697. Known as the Leedsville Hotel in the 1800s, it was a stop on the Lakewood–New York stagecoach route. The inn was famous for serving its pure well water that revitalized travelers. One can only wonder if those weary passengers indulged in more potent drinks as well.

THE STATE'S OLDEST WINERY

The development of New Jersey champagne and other wines is credited to Master Vintner Louis Nicholas Renault (1822–1913), who represented the celebrated champagne house of the duke of Montebello in Rheims, France. The wine industry was thriving until a parasitic aphid known as phylloxera devastated the French vineyards in the mid-nineteenth century.

Renault sailed for America seeking better conditions for wine grapes in 1855. At first, he journeyed to California. Gold wasn't the only valuable resource in the West at that time. The availability of fertile land and good weather provided opportunities for vintners. But the phylloxera epidemic that had destroyed so many French vineyards was spreading in California too.

The resourceful Monsieur Renault didn't panic. He had heard about a native grape that grew on the East Coast of the United States that was resistant to the destructive aphid. Determined to succeed with his wines, Renault moved east to southern New Jersey, where the defiant grape was said to flourish. He found the climate and soil in the area to be similar to those of his homeland in France. In 1864, he settled in the Egg Harbor area and established his winery; in 1870, he began to market his New Jersey champagne.

Please Don't Chill the Tonic

In 1919, at the onset of prohibition, the Renault Winery was purchased by John D'Agostino, a successful grocery business owner and his family. While America was dry, the D'Agostino family continued to operate with a government permit that allowed them to produce wine for religious and medicinal purposes. Renault Wine Tonic, with an alcoholic content of 22 percent, became their most profitable product and was sold in drugstores. The curative drink bore a label that warned "not to chill the tonic, as it would turn into wine which is illegal."

In 1933, the age of flappers and bootlegging came to a close when prohibition was repealed. Now Renault didn't have to only sell limited amounts to drugstores. The company could expand its selections of wines to the drinking public.

Curiously, the infamous Atlantic City political boss of the Roaring Twenties, Enoch "Nucky" Johnson (his name crops up frequently) worked for the Renault Winery, but well after the raucous days of prohibition. In 1941, Nucky was sent to jail for tax evasion. His wife, Flo, a former showgirl, worked at the Renault Winery gift shop while Nucky was incarcerated, and he allegedly was employed there as a salesman for a while after his release in 1945.

After John D'Agostino died in 1948, his sister, Maria, took over the winery and transformed it into a showplace that lured visitors. In 1966,

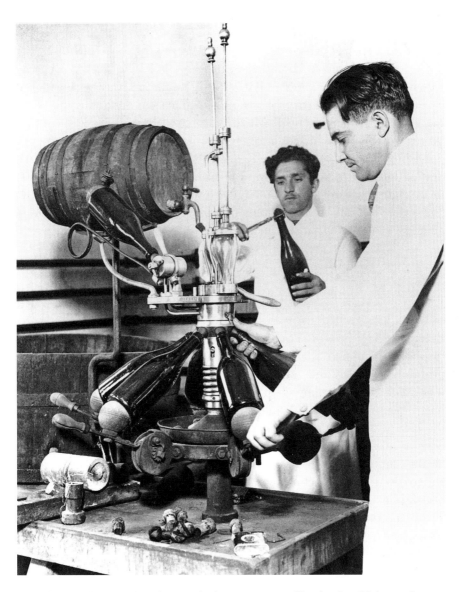

At the Renault Winery: "American made champagne—a million bottles of it is stored in the plant at Egg Harbor and the managers of the establishment, who claim that they already have orders for all of it, have placed the plant under heavy guard to thwart any ambitious attempts of hijackers to get in on the champagne market with the actual repeal of Prohibition." *International News Photo, October 23, 1933.*

she added a wineglass museum to display her exquisite glasses that date back to the thirteenth century. Her collection can still be viewed by tourists in a special room at the Renault Winery.

In 1968, Universal Foods, a worldwide distributor, took over the winery until 1974, when MCC Presidential, a New Jersey–based investment group, became the owner. The place was not doing well when the current owner, Joseph P. Milza, purchased it in 1977. Drawing on his prior experience in retailing, the hospitality business and newspaper publishing, Milza turned the Renault Winery into a popular tourist destination with a tasting room, a gift shop and guided tours. In 2001, he built the Tuscany House Hotel and Joseph's Restaurant, and in 2004, Vineyard Golf, an eighteen-hole championship golf course, was added adjacent to the 1,400-acre winery.

AFTER PROHIBITION

Before 1933, farmer Frank Tomasello was growing peaches and raspberries on his Atlantic County farm in Hammonton, but when prohibition ended, he seized the opportunity to produce grapes for wine. The winery began when Tomasello obtained one of the first New Jersey liquor licenses issued after prohibition. The winery has stayed in the family, as Frank's sons ran the business, and now third-generation winemakers John K. Tomasello and Charles Tomasello Jr. are carrying on the family tradition. Their wines run the gamut from Atlantic county Ranier Red to European favorites such as Chardonnay and Cabernet Sauvignon to wines made from locally grown cranberries and blueberries. Today, according to its brochure, the Tomasello Winery is the largest wine-producing business in the state and operates five outlets that offer wine tastings.

FROM FARMHOUSE TO MODERN CATERING BUSINESS

In the 1930s, despite the depression, restaurants were opening up at various locations along the coast, not only at the big resorts. Tory and Ida

Kawamoto, who operated a restaurant on Broadway and Ocean Avenue in Long Branch, decided to buy a farmhouse from C.E. Anderson on Monmouth Road in West Long Branch. In the early 1930s, it was still a rather bucolic area just off the now busy Route 36 with its strip malls and office complexes. Tory remodeled the old home as a restaurant and built a serene Japanese garden, with a fishpond and waterfall by the entrance.

Tory's was open until about 1941, when Ida became ill and Tory was slated to be placed into a Japanese internment camp. Sadly, rather than be confined to a camp, Tory committed suicide by hanging himself outside E.C. Hazard's Hospital in Long Branch in 1942. Ida died the following year.[35]

Belgian-born Joseph Damon bought Tory's restaurant, remodeled it and called it Joseph's. He specialized in wedding receptions and banquets. When Damon first came to America, he worked as a butler at the Long Branch estate of a wealthy New York shirt maker. His wife was employed as a maid and her mother as the cook.[36] Joseph's restaurant did well during the 1950s and 1960s and then changed hands in 1972. The site became Squire's Pub, a popular restaurant owned by Basil Plasteras, but it needed updating by the close of the twentieth century. In 2002, Squire's Pub was sold and became Branches, an upscale catering business. Under the direction of seasoned hospitality executive John Lombardo, the facility was transformed into an elegant event venue and reception hall that is in business today.

THE CELEBRATED COOKS OF THE CHALFONTE

Outstanding southern cuisine is a trademark of Historic Cape May's oldest continuously operating hotel, the Chalfonte. With its gingerbread trim and traditional porch rockers, this enchanting establishment appears to be frozen in time. Originally built in 1876 by Civil War Union colonel Henry Sawyer, it was later operated for over sixty years by the Satterfields, a Richmond, Virginia family with Confederate ties. This blending of traditions has made the Chalfonte a unique destination "where the South meets the North."

Several generations of African American women from a Virginia family have been employed at the Chalfonte, from the early twentieth century through to the present day. Clementine Young, who would come up from Virginia with the Satterfields every summer, was the head chambermaid. She first brought her daughter, Helen, with her in 1923. Helen eventually worked as a babysitter for the Satterfield children, then as a waitress, eventually becoming the head waitress. When the regular cook for the Chalfonte's Magnolia Room left, Helen Dickerson was asked to fill in, and she ended up becoming the head chef, a position she held for more than thirty years. Her daughters, Dot and Lucille, worked summers at the Chalfonte, and eventually they both joined their mother in the kitchen. Helen passed away in 1991. Dot Burton and Lucille Thompson, who learned southern cooking from their mother, continued working at the Chalfonte. The ladies' culinary delights, including their famous crab cakes, are prepared in the hotel's kitchen and served in the famous Magnolia Room.

In 1986, the Chalfonte published a book of Helen Dickerson's recipes that included some of Dot's specialties as well. The title, *I Just Quit Stirrin' When the Tastin's Good*, is a quote from the awe-inspiring chef Helen. She agreed that it was time for her recipes to be written down. The directions for buttermilk biscuits, black-eyed peas with hamhock, pigs feet, eggplant casserole and pecan pie are treasures. The Chalfonte crispy fried chicken is legendary. In the cookbook, Dot wrote that before adding chicken to oil in the skillet, "Throw in thickly sliced onion rings when grease is hot—that's our secret!" Vintage utensils dangle from hooks, and the same huge cast-iron frying pan that Helen first cooked with is still in the Chalfonte kitchen.

Helen appeared on *The Phil Donohue Show* and with her daughters and was featured on *Tyler's Ultimate* on the Food Network. The chefs of the Chalfonte have appeared countless times in the media over the years. Today, Dot and Lucille, in their eighties and still cooking at the Chalfonte, are simply referred to as "the ladies."

THE BEGINNINGS OF FAST FOOD

It's hard to say exactly when fast-food places began at the Jersey Shore. The concept seems to have evolved over a long period of time, although it wasn't generally called "fast food" until sometime in the mid-twentieth century.

So, what exactly is it? The term can mean several different types of eateries and quick meals that can be purchased from a small cart, a drive-in, a take-out shop or an informal restaurant with counters or tables. Street vendors and food carts even existed in ancient civilizations. In colonial America, city streets had plenty of "fast food" for sale.

Along the Jersey coast, outdoor vendors sold food to visitors and local fishermen long before the boardwalks were built. A freed slave known as "Vinie" reportedly operated an early "cake stand" at Cape May. Manumitted in 1803, Vina Armour was born in about 1771. Her husband froze to death after getting drunk, but she survived through the Revolutionary War, the War of 1812, the Mexican-American War and the Civil War. She died in about 1869 at about ninety-eight years. At her popular food stand, the well-loved Vinie also sold "purge beer," a drink made from herbs and barks that were "selected and gathered by her, being quite bitter and purgative."[37]

Carhops and Drive-Ins

In the Roaring Twenties, America's love affair with the automobile created new venues for food and entertainment entrepreneurs. With increased mobility came more freedom, more privacy and a new breed of teenagers. By the 1930s, young people were crazy about the new "drive-ins." These roadside restaurants were fast and inexpensive, and drive-in movies were also a big hit, with the first one opening in 1933 near Camden.

During the Great Depression, few teens could afford their own automobile, but they begged mom and pop for the family car keys—and often got their request. The new restaurants, with their delicious sandwiches and sodas, began to crop up along the Jersey coast.

Years before any golden arches appeared, the shore drive-ins had some similar choices to today's fast-food places, but vintage menus show many outdated selections. Cheeseburgers and fries have endured, but Celia Brown's depression-era menu also lists a "Pineapple with Cream Cheese" sandwich for twenty cents.

Just as fast food establishments today are scrambling to offer healthy choices, the individually owned drive-ins of the depression era offered

Our Pledge

——o——

All products used by us are the best that can be produced.

For making our Ice Cream the best ingredients are used—regardless of cost. We do not believe better or more wholesome Ice Cream is made. Take a quart with you. Enjoy our Ice Cream in your home.

You can also enjoy our sandwiches and Fried Chicken in your own home. Put up convenient to take out.

In selecting and handling our meats utmost care is used.

It is our desire to render pleasing service.

Please report any discourtesies on the part of attendants.

CELIA BROWN'S

Celia Brown's
DELICIOUS SANDWICHES

Drive In

UNION, N. J.
Three blocks North of Union Center
1259 Stuyvesant Avenue

BELMAR, N. J.
Main Street at 18th Avenue

ASBURY PARK, N. J.
1313 Asbury Avenue

This page and opposite: A late 1930s menu from Celia Brown's Belmar drive-in.

DELICIOUS SANDWICHES

Barbecue Pig	.15	Bacon, Lettuce and Tomato	.30
Hamburger	.15	Pineapple with Cream Cheese	.20
Onion or Relish		Lettuce and Tomato	.20
Cheeseburger	.20	Cream Cheese with Jelly	.15
Special	.25	Cream Cheese on Date and	
Barbecue, Lettuce and Swiss Cheese		Nut Bread	.15
Steak	.25	Swiss Cheese with Lettuce	.15
Onion or Relish		Toasted Cheese	.15
Bacon and Lettuce	.25		

Whole Wheat Bread on Request

HOT PLATES

60c

Steak Plate	.40	Half Fried Chicken	.50
Tender chicken fried Steak, French fried Potatoes, Tomato, Lettuce, Buttered Toast		Half fried Chicken, French fried Potatoes, Lettuce, Tomato, Buttered Toast.	
Scrambled Eggs and Toast	.25	Bacon and Eggs	.40

French Fried Potatoes .... .10

SALADS

Pineapple and Cream Cheese	.20	Tomato and Lettuce	.20

Fruit Salad with whipped cream   .20

FOUNTAIN DRINKS

"We make the best Chocolate Ice Cream Soda in the World or any other place"

Ice Cream Sodas	.20	Orangeade	.15
Chocolate, Lemon, Coffee, Pineapple, Strawberry		From fresh, choice fruit	
Sundaes	.20	Lemonade—made our way	.15
Walnut Sundae	.25	Tomato Juice	.10
Hot Fudge Sundae	.25	Coffee	.10
Malted Milks	.20	With pure cream	
Chocolate, Lemon, Coffee, Pineapple, Strawberry		Tea .... .10 Coca Cola	.05
Egg Malted Milk	.25	Milk—Grade A	.10
Chocolate Milk	.15	Root Beer, large glass	.10
With whipped cream		Canada Dry Ginger Ale, sm. .10; lg.	.25
Hot Chocolate	.10	Seven Up .... small .10; lg.	.25

ICE CREAM

Our All Cream Ice Cream is a Real Health Food—Take a Quart Home—.65

Chocolate, Strawberry, Vanilla, Butter Pecan, Raspberry Ice

| Dish .15 | Quart .65 | Pint .35 | Half Pint .20 | Cones .10 |

YOU CAN ENJOY SOME OF OUR ITEMS IN YOUR OWN HOME — PUT UP CONVENIENT TO TAKE OUT. SUCH AS SANDWICHES, FRIED CHICKEN, ICE CREAM, ETC.

Celia Brown's drive-ins were in Union, Asbury Park and Belmar. The Belmar and Asbury Park staff posed for this group photo in 1937 at Belmar. Owner Mrs. Condé McGinley (her maiden name was Celia Brown) is in the front row with her dog, Jack. This location at the southwest corner of Eighteenth and F Streets would later become Huhn's Drive-In and eventually the home of radio station WRAT.

Joe Long of Bayonne loved being a carhop at Celia Brown's Asbury Park restaurant in the late 1930s. However, during World War II, Long had to leave the job, and he became a lieutenant commander as a navy frogman in the Pacific.

some alternatives to the fattier foods such as the "Barbecue Pig." At Celia Brown's, you could order a tomato and lettuce salad, fruit salad (but suggested with whipped cream) and fresh fruit orangeade. The menu claimed, "Our All Cream Ice Cream Is a Real Health Food." Take-out was not yet common, but it was starting to catch on. Celia Brown's offered sandwiches to go, and ice cream could be purchased by the quart.

Raymond Davis started working at Celia Brown's in 1936. He was eighteen years old, and he enjoyed the job. No wonder, since he made good money in tips, "as much as $50 a night," an incredibly large amount for a young man, or anyone, during that era. Ray worked his way up quickly and became manager of the Belmar shop from 1938 to 1941. He described the burgers as big and juicy, with a "special" sauce that combined ketchup and mustard, served on custom rolls.

The majority of seasonal workers were college students from various areas but mostly Pennsylvania. According to Davis, the drive-ins were busy hangouts until 3:00 a.m. Many of the young men who worked at Celia Brown's entered the armed forces in the Second World War. Ray became a captain with the First Armored Division in North Africa and in Italy.[38]

America needed to ration food, and much of the workforce was at war, though women at home took on jobs formerly done by men, including those in the food service industry. As the war raged on, carhop jobs went to young women. Some people today remember carhops at the shore as attractive females on roller skates, like the iconic one on the poster for the 1973 film *American Graffiti*.

Drive-ins and burger places began to spring up all over the highways leading to shore resorts, and by the mid-1950s, major chain fast-food restaurants were being frequented, but these places that mushroomed across the nation are not the focus of this book, which concentrates on the privately run establishments and small regional chains. The Circus Drive-In on Route 35 represents a pioneering and independent fast-food restaurant. Established in 1954, it's a fun, family-owned, one-of-a-kind place that's still in business today.

COMFORT FOOD

Horse-drawn lunch wagons dating to the 1880s are often considered to be the first "diners," but the diner as we think of it today, a stationary silver boxcar-style haven for comfort food, has its roots in New Jersey. Jerry O'Mahoney of Bayonne manufactured prefabricated diners at his factory in Elizabeth from about 1917 to the 1950s. "From the 1920s to the 1980s, New Jersey had at least six and as many as twenty manufacturers churning out long, narrow, modular, railroad-style diners with curved roofs, squat windows, and enameled porcelain exteriors."[39]

Diners were opened up all over roadside New Jersey. The majority of them are located on the main corridors of north, central and southwestern areas of the state, but the coast has its diners too. The Monmouth Queen Diner in Asbury Park and the Neptune Diner on Routes 33 and 35 were constructed by the Kullman Company in the 1960s.[40] Many Greek immigrants opened diners, and some became full-service restaurants with a bigger variety of meals on the menu than the original diners had—some even with bars.

Entire books and websites are devoted to diners, so it's hard to choose one example at the Jersey Shore, but Mustache Bill's at Barnegat Light on Long Beach Island epitomizes the classic silver 1950s style diner. It was once called Joe's Barnegat Diner. Current owner Bill Smith started there as a dishwasher at the age of fourteen, returned, bought the business in 1972 and has operated it ever since…and yes, he does have a mustache. Smith has kept up traditional diner food on the menu, including his signature chipped beef. He makes a special "Cyclops" pancake with a fried egg for the eye and pancakes in whimsical shapes such as mermaids or whales for kids. Guy Fieri has featured Mustache Bill's diner on his Food Network show *Diner's, Drive-Ins and Dives*, and it won the coveted James Beard Award in 2009.

Shore eateries did exceptionally well in the 1930s considering the economic state of the nation. Things were looking up, but then new challenges arose during the Second World War. The New Jersey coast was under a state of alert, on the lookout for German U-boats. Blackouts were frequent, and big resort hotels became temporary barracks for soldiers waiting to be deployed. Military personnel and their families enjoyed the beach, boardwalks and eateries, but usually the fare was simple.

ZABERER'S WONDERFUL WORLD

During the 1950s and 1960s, although fast food was on the rise, families sometimes wanted a nice sit-down meal, a "Sunday style" dinner. The two Jersey Shore restaurants opened by the Zaberer brothers fit the bill for homey yet stylish dining.

It all began in the 1920s, when Frances Zaberer, a Wildwood restaurant and hotel owner, opened a place called Hollidays. Her two sons, Charles and Ed, helped their mom at Hollidays, but by the 1930s, each one had their own hot dog stand. In 1955, the Zaberer family purchased a restaurant in North Wildwood that became Zaberer's Anglesea Inn. But the two brothers didn't get along and parted ways, though both stayed in the restaurant business. Charlie and his wife, Rita, went to Atlantic City and started their own Zaberer's on the Black Horse Pike near the Atlantic City Racetrack, while Ed and his wife, Ayne, continued with the restaurant in North Wildwood.

Opening its doors in 1961, Charlie Zaberer's on the Black Horse Pike in Egg Harbor Township was a huge establishment, popular for weddings and banquets, that seated about 1,200 and at its peak had about 350 employees. After Charles' death in 1971, Rita ran the restaurant until 1983.

At Wildwood, Ed, a promotional genius, put his image on ads and matchbook covers, calling himself "The Host of the Coast." Eminent people dined there, including Richard M. Nixon and Ronald Reagan. Zaberer's served big portions with huge slabs of prime ribs, stuffed baked potatoes and fresh baked rolls. There was a special kids menu, and Ed Zaberer would pose for photos with children on his lap in an antique barber chair located in the lobby. In 1987, Ed sold his famous restaurant to a New York City businessman who auctioned off the contents in 1991. The building was destroyed by a fire in 1992.

Many still remember both of the Zaberer's restaurants, and there's nothing quite like them today. How can anyone forget sayings like "Get Zaberized" or drinking giant "Zaberized Cocktails"?

Stuffed Baked Potatoes

Unfortunately, most of the Zaberer's recipes were not written down, but in her book *Wildwood By-the-Sea: Nostalgia & Recipes*, author Anita Hirsch used her culinary expertise to provide this one from her memory. Stuffed baked potatoes were popular, especially with the prime ribs (which were said to be so big that they would hang over the edge of the plate).

6 Idaho or baking potatoes
3 tablespoons butter
3 tablespoons milk
⅛ teaspoon garlic powder
⅛ teaspoon salt
2 egg whites, stiffly beaten
2 tablespoons grated cheese (parmesan, pecorino or cheddar)
paprika

Wash and scrub the potatoes. Oil the potatoes with your favorite cooking oil using a pastry brush, or just oil your hands and rub them over each potato. Place the potatoes on a baking sheet and bake at 425 degrees for 30 minutes. Remove the tray from the oven and pierce each potato with a fork to allow the steam to escape. Place the tray back into the oven and bake another 20–30 minutes or until the potatoes are tender.

Allow the potatoes to cool enough to handle them. Cut a thin slice of skin off the top of each potato, wide enough so you can scoop out the insides. Place the insides of the potatoes in a bowl and place the empty skins on a baking sheet. Have the stiffly beaten egg whites nearby. Then heat the butter and milk together in a small microwavable bowl until the butter is just melted. Beat the butter and milk mixture into the potato pulp with the garlic powder and salt. Beat until fluffy and no lumps remain. Fold the stiffly beaten egg white into the potato mixture.

Fill the potato skins with the potato mixture. There will be extra potato, which you can place in a pastry bag to decorate the top of the stuffed potatoes. Top each potato with about a teaspoon of the grated cheese and some paprika. Place the potatoes back into a 400-degree oven until golden brown or place about eight inches under the broiler, just until the cheese is golden.

Tip: If you stuff the potatoes early in the day or cover and refrigerate the day before, you can heat and brown the potatoes in a 400-degree oven until brown about 20 minutes just before serving. Serves 6.

Courtesy of Anita S. Hirsch.

FROM TABLE TO FINGERS

The nature of Jersey Shore food went through major transformations during the course of the twentieth century. The enormous structured meals of the old Victorian hotels had gradually given way to simpler and quickly prepared meals and fast-food restaurants. There were some exceptions and things would change, with gourmet dishes having become more prevalent again in recent years. But perhaps the foods most people think of as being representative of the seashore are hand-held or finger foods, the kind you can eat while you are walking the boardwalks or relaxing on the beach.

Casual Eats and Boardwalk Treats

Tasty Recollections

Memories of casual eating at the Jersey Shore never really fade. The sights, smells and flavors of the foods are vividly recalled. People love to reminisce about past times at the shore, and their mouths water for the things they loved to eat. Incredibly, many of those foods and classic eateries are still around.

Vicki Gold Levi, well-known author and Atlantic City historian, grew up in the "Playground of the Nation" and lived there year round. Her father, Al Gold, was Atlantic City's chief photographer from 1939 to 1964. Vicki met the stars, served as a page for Miss America and, of course, she knew "Mr. Peanut." She frolicked on the Steel Pier as if it were summer camp, leaving her lunch on the open deck and never worrying that anyone would take it or spike it with anything unpleasant. Vicki recently recounted her memories of Atlantic City food:

> *Each local beach resort has its own special morsels that define its casual reputations. Atlantic City certainly has its share, and these are the ones I fondly remember from my youth: Subs, not hoagies, but subs or submarine sandwiches were made even tastier because the bread was made with water from our artesian wells. The bread was incomparable and unduplicated anywhere that I have ever been. Most memorable was the amazing cheese*

steak from the legendary and still standing White House Subs, but another favorite of mine was the creamy tuna from the now defunct Super Sub Shop. For me a sub wasn't complete without some sort of Tastykake plastic-wrapped commercial chocolate covered pastry for dessert, washed down with a cold glass of Kligerman's milk. Taylor Pork Roll was a special Boardwalk treat, and the succulent pork on its own special roll was always a must. Fralinger's and James' Salt Water Taffy are known all over the world, but I would drool for a Fralinger's almond macaroon cookie, and still crave them! Kohr's swirly soft ice cream was not just Atlantic City's, but nevertheless a Boardwalk must, as well as peanuts in the shell from Planters. Special occasions were celebrated with lobsters you picked out yourself from a giant vat of see-through water at Hackney's or the sweetest delicious clams at the Knife and Fork Inn (an eatery still happily with us). Special brunches would include miniature blueberry pancakes at The Jem, juicy hamburgers on a beach break at Hi Hat Joe's and then we all went back to the sand and waited for the guy to come around with his portable freezer on a shoulder strap shouting, "Come and get your fudgcicles and orange icicles!" Deli delectables after Saturday dates would surely be shared, a pastrami or roast beef sandwich at Kornblau's or pizza at Tony's Baltimore Grill, and the sweet taste of fudge from Steel's still lingers in my mouth. As the song says, "These are a few of my favorite things."

PIZZA: "THAT'S AMORE"

In 1953, Dean Martin crooned, "When the moon hits your eye like a big pizza pie, that's amore." Pizza was already well liked in the United States, but this song from the Dean Martin/Jerry Lewis movie *The Caddy* made the nation go pizza crazy. American troops who were stationed in Italy during World War II came home with a desire for pizza, and Italian-American celebrities (who frequented the Jersey Shore) such as Joe DiMaggio and Frank Sinatra contributed to the food's popularity.

Pizza's origins go back to ancient civilizations, and historians have various explanations as to how the first pizza was made by the Greeks or Romans—or anyone who created flat, round bread and cooked it on a hot stone. Tomatoes were added when they were brought back to Europe from South America in the sixteenth century. Interesting stories of the development of this beloved food abound, but for this book—we need to fast-forward to New Jersey in the early twentieth century.

After going through the rigors of Ellis Island, many Italian immigrants who settled in New Jersey found jobs related to the food industry as cooks, butchers, bakers and farmworkers. These hardworking people brought their fine cuisine and insistence on fresh ingredients with them. Some started their own farms, and a number of them opened Italian restaurants, bakeries and grocery stores throughout the Garden State. Many made the coast their home.

TOMATO PIES

Trenton, the state capital, is known for its tomato pies, said to have originated in about 1910. Before that time, the true tomato pie had no cheese. Some people use the names "tomato pie" and "pizza" interchangeably, but others maintain that they are not the same. The difference between a tomato pie and a pizza is that the cheese goes first on the tomato pie, followed by the sauce on top. The Garden State is the ideal place for fresh tomatoes, so it's not surprising that the dish became popular in the state. The crust of a Trenton tomato pie is thin, and most New Jersey and New York versions feature thin crusts.

Pizza, as most people know it today, is made with the tomato sauce first and then the cheese (usually mozzarella) on top so that it becomes gooey and is fun to eat, especially when it's stringy. Pizza became one of those foods that people loved to eat on boardwalks, at a stand with a soda or at a bar with a beer. But the pies are versatile and can also be served at nice sit-down restaurants with salad and wine. Pepperoni, mushrooms and peppers have become favorite add-on toppings. But modern pizza is not always made with tomato sauce, and many variations exist, such as the "white" style without tomato sauce. A variety of creative toppings are available, and pizzas can be veggie, organic or artisan. They can have whole grain crusts and other options.

So where was the very first pizza (or tomato pie) served at the Jersey Shore? It's an impossible question to answer exactly. However, there are some pizza parlors that are still in business and have been family owned for sixty years or more. A few of these historic places are described here; there are even more with tasty pizzas and/or tomato pies. They are divided geographically here, but there is no particular difference between pizza in the northern or southern regions of the Jersey coast.

Pizzerias at the North Jersey Shore

Sam Aldarelli is said to have made Asbury Park's first tomato pie on Ridge Avenue during the early 1920s.[41] Sam, a baker, gave up his regular job to sell pizza at his restaurant that he named for his wife, Freda. Sam was the great-uncle of the current owner Nicholas Aldarelli. In 1945, Nicky's grandfather, Papa Nick, and his wife, Letizia, purchased the Market Tavern on Fifth Avenue in Neptune and renamed it Mom's Kitchen, a restaurant that's popular today.

Pete and Elda's Bar, home of Carmen's Pizza on Route 35 in Neptune City, is a favorite casual shore eatery that always attracts a crowd. The popular bar has been at its current site since the 1930s under several different names, until Pete Vanola and his wife, Elda, purchased it in 1953. Carmen Andretta opened an Italian restaurant in conjunction with the Vanolas bar in about 1961. Carmen developed an original recipe for exceptionally thin pizza crust that became a big hit and is enjoyed today. The present owner, George Andretta, Carmen's son, started working at the restaurant as a kid in the 1960s. He took over for his father in 1979 and purchased the bar from the Vanolas in 1984. In recent decades, the restaurant has begun a tradition that if you are able to eat an entire extra-large pizza by yourself, you get a free T-shirt. Besides pizza, it offers an extensive menu of Italian-American cuisine.

Vittoria "Vic" Giunco and his wife came to the United States from Genoa, Italy, looking for a better life and hoping to raise a family. They settled in Bradley Beach in the 1910s and had two children. Vic tried operating a fruit stand and a candy shop, but neither business worked out. At the close of prohibition in 1933, Vic opened a bar called Vic's Tap Room on Main Street in Bradley Beach. Despite the depression, business was booming, and in about 1940, he was able to purchase more property on the south end of town. He moved the bar down the street to where Vic's Italian-American Restaurant is located today at 60 Main Street. Vic's son, John, added the restaurant to the bar in 1947. The family has carried on the tradition with not only delicious pizza but also a variety of Italian-American dishes. When John passed away in 2001, his daughter and son-in-law took over, and now their children are involved in the family business that all began with two immigrants from Genoa who followed their dreams.[42]

In historic Long Branch, Freddie's Restaurant and Pizzeria moved in 1952 to its present location at 563 Broadway from across the street, where it first began in 1944. The founder, Fred Scialla, worked as an Italian baker and developed a unique pizza dough recipe for thin-crust pies. He owned the Long Branch restaurant and one that was located in Asbury Park. In 1995, Mark A. Brockriede (Freddie's great-nephew) purchased the business. Freddie's today features its famous thin-crust pizza and offers a variety of Italian dishes. Celebrities—including members of the E-Street band—have been regular customers. Danny DeVito once had a Freddie's pizza delivered to him in Pennsylvania while he was working on a movie.[43]

Another classic Italian restaurant is Vesuvio at 705 Tenth Avenue in Belmar. Established in 1937, it has been continuously owned and operated by the same family all these years. Vesuvio specializes in pizza and other Italian dishes, including soups, eggplant and mussels. It is also known for its famous cheesecake to top it all off. The comfy décor of the place, with its turquoise Naugahyde booths, hasn't changed in decades.

PIZZERIAS AT THE SOUTH JERSEY SHORE

At Seaside Park today, there's the legendary Maruca's Tomato Pies, which began in 1950 with four enterprising brothers in Trenton. After the untimely death of their father, they decided that there was no future in working the Pennsylvania coal mines, as he had done for so many years before moving to Trenton in the 1930s. Anthony, Pasquale, Joseph and Dominick Maruca decided on a tomato pie business and opened shops at the busy Jersey Shore. They had several locations on the Seaside Heights Boardwalk from 1950 to 1989. Maruca's at Seaside Park opened in 1955 after the devastating Freeman's Amusement Center fire destroyed three blocks of the boardwalk. Maruca's at Seaside Park, the only one of their shops remaining, is a thriving business today and is run by twins Dominic and Joe Maruca. Their signature pie, with its swirly design, looks like a work of art. A special cheese blend goes on first, and then the sauce is applied in a concentric circle on top.

Established in 1950, Maruca's Tomato Pies got its start in Trenton. The current shop on the Seaside Park Boardwalk (photographed here in 2012) has been open since 1955. It was featured on the Travel Channel's *Man v. Food* with Adam Richman.

Modern history was made when Travel Channel host Adam Richman of *Man v. Food* featured Maruca's on his show in 2010.

Another celebrated place for pizza, known as Mack and Manco's for years, is located in Ocean City. Anthony Mack and Vincent Manco came from Trenton to Ocean City in 1956 and opened a pizza parlor at 918 Boardwalk; within a few years, they had added a second place at Seventh Street and Boardwalk. Mack's three sons—Dominic, Vince and Joseph—opened businesses at the Wildwood and Atlantic City Boardwalks, while Manco's son, Frank, and his wife, Kay, continued the original Ocean City locations and opened another store at Twelfth Street in the late 1980s. The pies are consistently good, and loyal customers come back year after year. Today, their daughter, Mary, keeps the tradition going. The historic pizza business's new name as of 2012 is Manco & Manco. It's still on the Ocean City Boardwalk, but they also have a second shop in Somer's Point.

The pizza dough that contains Atlantic City's artesian well water is a key ingredient to the success of that city's pies. There are many outstanding pizza restaurants around the resort city, but there's one that has been in business for almost eighty years. The name of Tony's Baltimore Grill crops up whenever historic Italian-American eateries are mentioned. In the 1920s, during prohibition, the Tarsitano family opened the original Baltimore Grill on Connecticut Avenue. The restaurant was located in the inlet district of Atlantic City, an area that was notorious for bootlegging. In 1966, the restaurant moved downtown to 2800 Atlantic Avenue and added the name of the original owner's son, Tony. Besides pizza, the menu features delicious pasta dishes and seafood. Tony's is a popular spot with local workers as the prices are low and the food is exceptional.

These are some of the famous pizza places that have been in business for decades along the Jersey coast. But there are many, many more. Wildwood has Mack's Pizza, and Red Bank has The Brothers—both places go back to the 1950s. Pizza is subjective—everyone has a regional favorite, a special neighborhood place.

SHORE SANDWICHES

At the Jersey Shore resorts, sandwiches have been around since Victorian times, maybe even before, but they gained in status just after World War II. Especially remarkable are the long submarine-shaped rolls heaped with sausage and peppers or deli meats and fixings. Often associated with Italian-American eateries and street vendors, these sandwiches have acquired regional names such as hoagies (Philadelphia), heroes (New York) or grinders (New England), but at the Jersey Shore, they are usually known as subs.

Under the Boardwalk

In the early years of the twentieth century, a sandwich shop thrived under the Atlantic City Boardwalk at Virginia Avenue called Submarine Saul. Owner Saul's niece married the "Great Josh Freedman," who became well known for his subs. Josh recalled how ocean water would sometimes flood Saul's little stand under the boardwalk near the trolley tracks. His customers would shout, "This place at high tide is like a submarine, Saul!"[44]

In the late 1950s, Josh operated a downbeach sub shop at 9218 Ventnor Avenue, and in 1962, he opened a new place across from the Atlantic City High School at 3709 Ventnor Avenue. The Great Josh's is long gone, but some people still remember his signature sandwich that says it all: the Bellyfiller.

White House Subs

At the close of World War II, a young serviceman named Anthony Basile returned from the Philippines and wanted to open up an eatery in his beloved hometown, Atlantic City. The son of an Italian immigrant who worked as a cement finisher on some of the resort's famous old hotels, Anthony got his first food business experience working as a boy at an uptown sandwich shop. Soon after his return from the war, he found a building on Arctic Avenue in Atlantic City's Italian-American neighborhood known as "Ducktown." Its freshly painted white stucco made him think of "a little white house," and thus the name was born. He opened White House Subs in 1946. Two years later, Anthony's uncle Fritz Sacco became his business partner.

Their subs are chock full of first-rate ingredients, but it's the bread that makes them so special. White House Subs orders fresh bread that is delivered throughout the day from renowned city bakeries Formica's and Rando's. The excellence of Atlantic City bread can be credited to the skill of the bakers and that important artesian well water. The Kirkwood-Cohansey Aquifer system in the Pine Barrens provides pure water from underground sources that are fed by cedar tree roots. They lend acid to the water that keeps impurities out and makes for great bread dough.

Over the years, scores of famous people appearing in Atlantic City have been customers of White House Subs, and their autographed photos are all over the walls. Stars who enjoyed the big, mouthwatering subs included Frank Sinatra and the Beatles when they appeared at Convention Hall in 1964. Teen idol Frankie Avalon[45] from Philadelphia stopped in for a sub after his Steel Pier performance on Labor Day in 1962. "The word spread quickly and almost 500 teenagers charged the White House. Five cases of soda were sold in 15 minutes, three radio cars were called and it took 20 minutes for the youth to escape his fans."[46]

The Beatles prepare to devour a giant sandwich from White House Subs during the Fab Four's 1964 concert at Convention Hall, Atlantic City. *Courtesy of Vicki Gold Levi (from* 125 Years of Ocean Madness*) and used with permission of White House Subs.*

After Fritz Sacco passed away in the 1990s, Anthony Basile kept active at White House Subs until his death in 2008. Their families continue to run the iconic business. A branch shop serving their delicious subs opened at Trump's Taj Mahal in 2011. White House Subs has been visited by famous television chefs and has been featured on talk shows. Customers who line up outside the Arctic Avenue store will tell you that it's well worth the wait.

JERSEY MIKE'S

The remarkable submarine sandwich empire now called Jersey Mike's began as Mike's Subs, a humble mom and pop store in Point Pleasant that first opened in 1956. At the age of fourteen, a local high school student named Peter Cancro began to work at Mike's after school in the early 1970s and loved it. His brother had worked there the previous summer. During his senior year, the shop went up for sale, and the enterprising Peter approached his football coach, who was a banker, about acquiring Mike's sub shop. Seventeen-year-old Peter Cancro got the financing and purchased the business, and people were soon lining up to buy his subs. At seventeen, he wasn't even legally old enough to slice the meat, and yet he owned the store.

Cancro franchised the business in 1987, and today he's CEO of Jersey Mike's Franchise Systems Inc., which maintains its corporate headquarters in Manasquan. Peter Cancro, the Jersey Shore boy with a vision, now

This humble Jersey Mike's sub shop, which was opened in Point Pleasant during the 1950s, was the start of a phenomenal business that now has franchises nationwide. Peter Cancro (on left in this 1970s photo) purchased this shop when he was only seventeen. Today, he is the successful head of Jersey Mike's, an ever-growing company with its headquarters in Manasquan. *Courtesy of Jersey Mike's.*

oversees more than five hundred stores across the country, with shops in Colorado, Louisiana, California, South Carolina and many more states. People all over the country and around the world were requesting Jersey Mike's subs, so the company began shipping them out overseas, prompting expansion of its operations. Jersey Mike's stresses quality and conducts intensive training programs.

Despite the vast size of the business today, Cancro said, "We don't feel like a chain."[47] The company prides itself on not compromising and maintaining a small-town atmosphere going back to the roots of the original Mike's. The sandwiches, true central Jersey subs, are all "made to order." The bread, fresh baked daily, is cut all the way through, and red wine vinegar and oil are used for the "juice." Jersey Mike's participates in supporting charitable events and causes, giving much back to the community. It's a business that is a phenomenal slice of Jersey Shore food history and is still growing.

THIS LITTLE PIGGY

"New Jersey Sausage" was so well known in nineteenth-century America that the San Francisco Women's Cooperative included it in its 1883 cookbook. Juicy, plump rolls of processed meat made from pork, usually eaten for breakfast, have been around a long time and are still well loved, especially at Jersey Shore towns and in Philadelphia. A slice of pan-fried pork roll with a fried egg and melted cheese on a roll is a passion for devotees, who insist that it is *the* Jersey Shore breakfast.

Taylor Pork Roll

A tightly packed ground ham, somewhat like pork roll, is said to date back to the Battle of Trenton during the American Revolution, but this cannot be verified. Pork roll, though a generic name, is often known as Taylor Ham (the same product as Taylor Pork Roll). John Taylor of Trenton is credited with being the first to develop the food item in 1856. Taylor, a businessman and politician born in Trenton in 1836, started out as a grocery store clerk. The resourceful young man worked his way up in the pork and beef packing industry and organized the Taylor Provision Company in 1888. He served as a state senator and built the Taylor Opera House in Trenton. Taylor died in 1909, but his name lives on with his famous product, whether it's called Taylor Ham or Taylor Pork Roll.

In the 1950s, at the peak of its retail operations at the Jersey Shore, Taylor Pork Roll had eight sandwich shops, including three in Atlantic City, two in Cape May and one each at Wildwood, Seaside and Asbury Park. The last shop standing was the one in Cape May that closed when the operator retired in the early 1980s.

Pork roll can truly be called a New Jersey regional food. The product is sometimes compared to Spam or baloney, but pork roll enthusiasts know they're not the same and argue that they're not even similar. Nothing can really compare! The product was traditionally packaged in coarse cloth sacks, but today the ever-popular Taylor Pork Roll is sold in modern packaging.

A well-known and fun feature of the pork roll is the way people cut the slices to keep them from curling up while frying. Triangular wedges are removed from each slice, and the shapes that result are commonly called "Fireman's Badges"; only one wedge is called a "Pac-man."

The Taylor Pork Roll store, which was located on the Boardwalk at Kentucky Avenue, as it looked in the 1950s. It was one of the eight popular shops the company operated at the Jersey Shore. Pork roll is also called Taylor Ham. *Courtesy of Taylor Provisions.*

During the winter, in the early 1950s, a crowd of hungry customers jams the Taylor Pork Roll store at Kentucky Avenue in Atlantic City. Atlantic City was frequented by tourists in the winter months. *Courtesy of Taylor Provisions.*

George Washington Case

John Taylor did not make the only Jersey pork roll in nineteenth-century New Jersey. He had a competitor who also made a quality product that is sold today. In 1870, Belle Mead farmer and butcher George Washington Case developed his own recipe for pork roll and began selling it. At first, his company was called the Case Pork Pack Company, and it soon became a thriving business. An interesting fact about his product is that it was packed in corn husks. Eventually, these were replaced by vacuum-sealed packaging, and the company name became Case's Pork Roll. The business takes pride in its history of hickory smoking the meat. The Case Pork Roll Company operated several shops at Jersey Shore resort towns, but they are no longer open. The company sells wholesale, and retail orders can be placed from its website.

HOT DAWG!

Hot dogs, frankfurters or franks, whichever name you wish to call them, were not invented in the United States. Austrian and German immigrants who came to America during the nineteenth century brought their traditional wienerwurst and other sausages along, and the dogs evolved from them.

Though often associated with New York's Coney Island, ballgames and street vendors, hot dogs rank high as favorite casual and boardwalk foods in the Garden State. In North Jersey, deep-fried "rippers" and "Texas wieners" are favored, but at the shore, they are often Italian style and can be cooked in different ways. Hot dogs are sold all along the Jersey coast, and Long Branch is particularly well known for them.

Max's Famous Hot Dogs

In 1928, during the heyday of the Roaring Twenties, a businessman named Max Altman opened a small boardwalk restaurant at the north end of Long Branch. He appropriately called it Max's and worked with Milford Maybaum, who eventually bought the place from him in 1950. The new owner, known as "Mel" kept the name Max's, and soon Mel Maybaum was being called "Mr. Max."

The restaurant was seasonal, so Mel was able to head south in the winter to pursue his love of horse racing. He fell in love with an attractive woman named Celia Levy, a New York native, and they were married in 1967. It wasn't long before Celia was known to all as "Mrs. Max," and the lady became a driving force and a symbol of Max's Famous Hot Dogs. Mr. and Mrs. Maybaum operated the Long Branch restaurant in the summer and enjoyed Florida and their passion for horse racing during the winter.

The first Max's boardwalk restaurant was destroyed by fire in 1969. That same year, they opened a new one, still on the boardwalk but a little farther south. Mr. Max passed away in 1980, before the second restaurant met the same fate in 1984. But you couldn't hold Max's down, and the resilient business moved slightly inland when Celia Maybaum and her family purchased the Surf Lounge at 25 Matilda Terrace. It was previously a supper club with a notorious reputation, but the new owners had nothing to do with any of that. They changed the place entirely. The Maybaum family completely reconstructed the building, and it soon became known

The Max's Hot Dogs on the Long Branch Boardwalk that opened at this location in 1969 was not far from the original site. After a fire, the restaurant moved to its present location at 25 Matilda Terrace, where the tradition continues. *Courtesy of Max's Famous Hot Dogs.*

only for good food, drink and camaraderie. It remains the location of the restaurant today.

Celia, with her bold, "larger than life" personality, operated the restaurant as a modern place but with traditional values. Adding her own touches, Celia (the "Hot Dog Queen") was well known for manning her post by the cash register and for her delicious cheesecake. She's ninety-three at the time of this writing, and the institution she made famous continues with Mel's son, Robert "Bobby" Maybaum, his wife, Madeline, and daughters Jennifer and Michele running the restaurant. They keep the legacy alive.

The walls are decorated with memorabilia, including pictures of the old locations, vintage signs, framed newspaper articles and autographed photos of celebrity visitors. The gallery of notables includes Bruce Springsteen (who has a home in Rumson), Brian Williams (a Middletown resident), Frank Sinatra, Danny DeVito (originally from Asbury Park), Joan Rivers, John Travolta and Cardinal O'Connor (who may seem an unlikely customer but who loved the hot dogs; he made friends with Celia on his visit to the area in 1994). The customers have come from all over, even as far as Australia.

Max's, the little shop that started with just twenty-five seats, is now a two-hundred-seat seasonal restaurant. Foot-long Schickhaus quarter-pound dogs lavished with chili and cheese, fresh corn on the cob, fries, sweet potato fries and onion rings are popular menu items that have become traditions. Max's also offers burgers, fish sandwiches, ice cream and more. There's beer on tap and a full bar. Today, Jennifer and her husband, Jake, also operate Max's Famous Hot Dogs on Wheels, a state-of-the-art food truck.

The WindMill

A short distance away from Max's, there's a fabled hot dog stand that looks like it came right out of a Dutch Renaissance landscape painting…but painted red and serving fast food. The WindMill on Ocean Boulevard in West End (Long Branch) is the flagship location for a small chain of restaurants (there are nine of them as of June 2012, all located in New Jersey). The windmill-shaped structure on Ocean Boulevard in West End that opened in 1964 was the first one. Besides the juicy Sabrett hot dogs, the eatery is known for its burgers, fries and ice cream.

Leo Levine, wife Eleanor and his brother, Ed Levine, bought the restaurant in 1976 when it was called the Wind Mill Drive Inn. They opened a second location in Belmar three years later. Since then, WindMill Gourmet Fast Foods has expanded and is still growing, but none of the other locations is actually shaped like a windmill. Ed passed away first, and Leo died on July 3, 2012. Leo's long and successful restaurant career began when he worked as a busboy in the Catskill Mountains, and he was a manager of the first Howard Johnson franchise in the United States.[48] Over the years, Max's and the WindMill have been called amicable rivals. Indeed, they have some things in common, but they are two very different types of eateries. Max's is an individual family-owned restaurant that goes back to 1928; the WindMill that started in the 1960s is a family-owned franchise business. Max's has a wait staff and a full bar; the WindMill is self-serve, with tables on the upper deck (and they use Sabrett dogs).

The celebrated women of the two Long Branch places known for hot dogs, Celia Maybaum (Mrs. Max) and Eleanor Levine of the WindMill, have been compared to each other.[49] They are both fascinating ladies who know dozens of celebrities, and they both have strong personalities. The two eateries have each won numerous awards. In 2008, the chili cheese dogs at WindMill and Max's were both recognized by Martha Stewart on her TV show as two of the best dogs in her lineup of favorites.

From Mrs. Jay's to the Stone Pony

Ida and John Jacobs opened a little hot dog stand at Ocean and Second Avenue in Asbury Park back in 1922. Then, with their daughter, Jeanette, and son-in-law, Murray Weiner, the couple purchased the stand and property and made it into a restaurant they called Mrs. Jay's. Ida and John also opened Mrs. Jay's Beer Garden adjacent to the restaurant and sold 2 percent beer during prohibition. In 1933, they were one of the first restaurant owners in Asbury Park to acquire a liquor license. In later years, the outdoor beer garden would become a mecca for bikers.

Joal Leone worked at Mrs. Jay's restaurant in the 1960s. Ida's daughter, who ran the place at that time, insisted that the waitresses look clean and crisp, with no dark fingernail polish or dangling earrings. It was a popular and well-run family restaurant. Joal recalled, "Mrs. Weiner even made sure we'd place a sprig of fresh parsley on every plate!"

In 1965, the beer garden added go-go dancers. Mrs. Jay's suffered after a much-publicized 1968 incident in which a dancer allegedly wore a see-

Mrs. Jay's restaurant, Asbury Park, was a typical family restaurant when this photo was taken in the late 1950s, but the place achieved legendary status. Since 1974, it has been the site of The Stone Pony, a landmark of musical history.

through blouse and the police raided the place. The Weiner family sold the restaurant in the early 1970s but kept the beer garden for a while. Then Mrs. Jay's eatery was purchased and transformed into a bar and music venue known as The Stone Pony. The now world-famous Jersey Shore landmark opened on February 8, 1974. Southside Johnny and the Asbury Jukes was the original house band. The club served as a springboard for Bruce Springsteen and Jon Bon Jovi and for other stars' careers. The Stone Pony is alive and well and still rocks with great music today.

A CLASSIC BOARDWALK LUNCHEONETTE

Most food concessions at the Jersey boardwalks were mom and pop stores before the fast-food chains became predominant. In the early 1950s, Irving Granoff, who had worked as a salesman, leased the luncheonette at Belmar's Tenth Avenue Pavilion that was built in the 1940s. Irving, a local resident, turned the business into a family affair by employing every relative he could recruit, which included three generations of immediate and extended family. He also employed several local high school students to help cover the long hours and seven-day weeks.

The Tenth Avenue beach was one of Belmar's most crowded spots in the 1950s, and the luncheonette provided a welcome hangout for both families and teens during both the hot daytime and cool evening hours. There was a grill that was open to the boardwalk if you wanted to take out your food to eat on the beach. Inside, a counter with stools and several tables were available for those who wanted to get out of the sun. Many of the customers were regulars who liked to stop and chat with the owner. Irving prided himself on the high quality of the fast food he served. Some of the summer favorites included chicken in a basket, fried shrimp, hamburgers, hot dogs, French fries and homemade roast beef sandwiches. Soft drinks were popular, as were malted milkshakes and ice cream sodas. Also, a thirst quencher that sold well was Green Spot, a noncarbonated orange drink. Ice cream was always a hot weather favorite with both children and adults. Irving used only Dolly Madison ice cream because he believed it was the creamiest ice cream made.[50]

On Labor Day in 1963, the old Tenth Avenue Pavilion burned down; it was replaced with a new building that currently houses a retail store where

A Belmar luncheonette (on left) at the Tenth Avenue Pavilion in the 1950s.

the luncheonette run by Irving Granoff once provided hungry beachgoers with quality fast food.

SALT WATER TAFFY

Taffy existed long before the advent of salt water taffy. American taffy is a chewy candy made from sugar, sweetener, butter and flavorings—usually with salt but not always. It's famous for being stretched, unlike toffee, its traditional British counterpart, which is allowed to set and then usually cut into neat squares. Taffy pulls had become all the rage at fairs and parties and in home kitchens in America by the mid-nineteenth century. Victorian children delighted in stretching ropes of taffy as a fun game.

The first salt water taffy is attributed to the Atlantic City Boardwalk in its early years. The name has helped to identify it with the Jersey Shore even though it is sold in some other states as well. Perhaps the most endearing food legend of New Jersey is the tale of how salt water taffy accidentally got its name.

When Atlantic City's first boardwalk (an innovation to keep sand from being tracked into hotels) was introduced in 1870, it was only eight feet wide and a mile long. New and improved walks replaced it over the years. Today, the Atlantic City Boardwalk is sixty feet wide and four miles long. Even back in the nineteenth century, enterprising retailers knew that it provided a fine venue for shops and amusements. Although Atlantic City was conceived as a health resort, people craved sweets and treats—fun things to eat while strolling or to take home as souvenirs.

As more tourists came, an increasing number of retail businesses popped up along the boardwalk. One merchant, who owned a small candy shop, suffered a hardship during a storm in 1883. At that time, the boardwalk was not far above sea level. As the story goes, the candy shop owner's stock of sweets was drenched in salt water after waves leaped up onto the low boardwalk. When vacationers could return following the storm, a little girl came into the man's shop and asked for taffy. The merchant chuckled and offered her some "salt water taffy." The girl, not understanding his sarcasm, bought some and told her friends about it. The owner's mother, who was in the back of the store, overheard the conversation and told her son to keep the name of salt water taffy—it would sell better! And so it did. Like most legends, this one has slightly different versions, but all of them suggest that the taffy was fortuitously soaked with salt water. The name turned out to be pure marketing genius.

Fralinger: The Salt Water Taffy King

Joseph Fralinger, the Atlantic City candy entrepreneur, wore many hats in his climb to success. He was born in 1848 in Atlantic County, New Jersey, where he learned the trade of glassblowing, but due to labor disputes, he moved to Philadelphia. He got married and worked as fishmonger selling oysters. He also played baseball and eventually managed a team. When his wife became ill, they went to Atlantic City to improve her health. Fralinger ran some popular baseball clubs in Atlantic City but then lost his money on a losing team. He took a lowly job as a hod carrier with a bricklayer and then discovered the emerging possibilities of shore resort enterprises. He opened a cigar store but then leased space for a fresh fruit and soft drink stand from Captain John L. Young. He sold apples, cider, mineral water and lemonade. Stories are told of how he juggled lemons to attract customers.

In 1884, Captain John L. Young asked Fralinger if he'd like to run the taffy stand on the Applegate Pier. Fralinger recognized the future of this confection and used his ingenuity to make delicious taffy. His first flavor was molasses, but he soon added chocolate and vanilla.

Fralinger's had a dynamic advertising campaign in the 1920s, with ads appearing in magazines and newspapers. A typical ad for Fralinger's Salt Water Taffy in the 1923 *Saturday Evening Post* used this slogan: "Sea air and sunshine are sealed in every box." If the taffy was not available in your hometown stores, it could be ordered and shipped directly to you from Atlantic City. Customers were cautioned to buy only genuine Fralinger's, "the long kind," to be sure of quality, purity and freshness.

Candy Maker Enoch James

Confectioner Enoch James said that he had been making a salt water taffy product for years in the Midwest. James and his sons moved to Atlantic City in about 1880. The clever candy maker revolutionized the industry. He created "cut to fit the mouth" taffy shapes and packed it in clever papier-mâché barrels and satchel containers that made great souvenirs.

In 1947, the Glaser family bought the James' Salt Water Taffy operation in Atlantic City. Frank Glaser, president of the company today, and his family are fifth-generation candy makers. Glaser's great-grandfather was a candy maker from Germany who immigrated to the United States in the nineteenth century and opened candy and chocolate shops in Philadelphia.

Fralinger and James were known to be rivals. Even long after they had passed on, the two companies remained competitors until the 1990s, when Frank Glaser took over. Today, the Glaser family carries on the traditions of the past while pioneering new methods of candy making. The Glaser family business today includes James' Salt Water Taffy, Fralinger's Salt Water Taffy and Bayard's Chocolate House, a company dating back to the 1930s that it recently acquired.

James' Salt Water Taffy, with seventeen flavors, is one inch long and "cut to fit the mouth," and Fralinger's, with sixteen flavors, is two inches long. Each brand is still made with its original and unique recipe. Today, the James Candy Company is the largest and most famous maker of premium salt water taffy, producing more than 600,000 pounds of salt water taffy each year. Other traditional treats made by the James Candy Company include its yummy macaroons and the popular peanut butter paddles, specialties that have delighted generations. The historic business has appeared in a number of television shows and movies. A Fralinger's Boardwalk store, circa 1920, was meticulously re-created in 2010 for the set of HBO's television series *Boardwalk Empire*.

Taffy was pulled by hand in the early days, but time-saving taffy-pulling machines were in use by the 1920s. This worker is at Fralinger's in Atlantic City, circa the 1930s or 1940s. *Courtesy of James Candy Company.*

SWEETS FOR THE SWEET

Every resort town along the Jersey coast has its own candy shops, and some of them have been around for a century or more. The aromas of freshly made fudge and caramel titillate the senses of vacationers. The rainbow hues of salt water taffy, Turkish delights and licorice swizzle sticks draw the eye to the candy stores. It would be hard to pass them by.

As described in an earlier chapter, candy did extremely well in the 1920s during prohibition. A number of confections that are popular today were first introduced during the Roaring Twenties, including Baby Ruth candy bars (named for President Cleveland's daughter, not the baseball player), Chuckles, Mounds, Mars, Milk Duds, Reese's Peanut Butter Cups and more. (M&M's, associated with New Jersey, were first produced by the Mars Company in Newark but not until 1941.)

Ocean City has its own famous candy business that is known for its brand of salt water taffy. In 1898, William F. Shriver opened Shriver's restaurant, ice cream and candy shop on the Ocean City boardwalk. Although there was a newsworthy but short-lived prohibition of candy sales on Sundays at Ocean City in the early 1920s, the candy businesses flourished. Four brothers who owned Dairy Maid Confectionery Company, a Philadelphia chain, purchased Shriver's in 1959, and it has stayed in the same family ever since.

Steel's Fudge, with a shop on the Atlantic City Boardwalk and one in Ocean City, was founded in 1919 by Elizabeth Steel. Her family carries on the business today selling rich, delicious fudge (as well as sugar-free fudge), salt water taffy, Kookaburro (black) licorice, "Steel's Brittle Peanut," butter toffee nuts and more.

Asbury Park had several well-known confectionery shops. Criterion Candies was opened by Louis Karagias in 1929 when it started out as a restaurant with a candy shop, eventually selling all candy. Criterion Chocolates, as it is known now, is in business today but is located in Eatontown. Leiding & Heinz confectioners was another popular seller of sweets in Asbury Park. Wildwood has Laura's Fudge, a short distance off the boardwalk, which has been in business since 1926. Laura's also has shops in North Wildwood, Ocean City and Cape May. Hankins Fudge, also off the boardwalk, was started by George and Mary Hankins in 1946. They started making candy in their garage and moved the business twice and then to its present location on Pacific Avenue.

"See the Mechanical Man in Our Windows." In the late 1950s, a child appears more interested in the candy than the "chef." Steel's Fudge still operates stores on the Atlantic City and Ocean City Boardwalks today.

The Fudge Kitchen in Cape May, owned by the Bogle brothers, has a long history. Joe Bogle began his career at the age of twelve when he had a summer job at Sagel's Candies on Beach Avenue. Harry Sagel's father, Louis, founded Sagel's Candies, and his first shop was started on the Wildwood Boardwalk in 1918. Joe Bogle got a job at Sagel's Cape May store in 1968 when Harry was in his eighties, and Harry taught him "everything he needed to know" about selling candy. In 1972, the Bogles opened their first store and five years later purchased Baxter's Candy Store, and they acquired Roth's Candyland in 1982. Both were Cape May shops dating back to the 1800s. The Bogles made fudge and invested in a vintage salt water taffy pulling machine.

A Recipe for Peanut Brittle

Nothing quite compares to buying candy at the seashore resorts, but for those who'd like to make old-time candy treats at home, here's a simple old recipe.

"Peanut Candy—Very Good. To six ounces of butter add a pound of light brown sugar and stir over a steady heat, cooking for ten minutes after the first bubble is seen. Add a cupful of peanuts rolled until like coarse crumbs. Spread in a buttered pan and mark off in squares at once."

From Mrs. Bawden's Freehold Cook Book, *Freehold, New Jersey, 1914. Special Collections and University Archives, Rutgers University Libraries.*

Nutty History

Peanuts are a popular boardwalk food associated with American tradition and sold at ball games and fairs. Planters, a well-known peanut company that's still going strong today, began in 1906 when a young Italian immigrant named Amedeo Obici and his friend Mario Peruzzi started a small business in Pennsylvania. It grew into the huge Planters nut company now based in Virginia. Mr. Peanut, an iconic figure in food advertising, was "born" in 1916 when a schoolboy submitted the winning logo of a peanut with arms and legs in a Planters contest. The top hat, monocle and cane were added later.

Planters' famous Atlantic City store, at Boardwalk and Virginia Avenue, first opened in 1930. The store that was popular for decades is no longer there. Visitors to the old Boardwalk store often recall how the debonair Mr. Peanut (a costumed person) would greet them. All sorts of novelties, such as cups and pens made with the image of Mr. Peanut, have been sold as souvenirs, and the older ones are now highly collectible. There were other Planters stores, including one at Times Square in New York. A statue of Mr. Peanut sits on a bench at the entrance to the Atlantic City History

Museum on the Garden Pier, and a vintage Mr. Peanut costume can be seen inside. An updated Mr. Peanut continues to be the company's mascot for advertising.

Famous Boardwalk Popcorn

Popcorn, another favorite snack, did not originate at the Jersey Shore; it goes back to ancient civilizations, became widespread in mid-nineteenth century America and has continuously gained in popularity. A well-loved movie snack, popcorn is also munched at fairs, amusement parks, ballgames and boardwalks. During the Great Depression, popcorn was one of the few affordable treats, and it was popular during World War II when sugar was rationed. With the rise of television in the 1950s, popcorn made its way into more homes.

Johnson's Popcorn, in business at the Jersey Shore since 1940, may have roots in 1920s Philadelphia. The tasty popcorn comes in several flavors, with caramel being the best seller over the years. It is still "hand mixed" in copper kettles, a process that draws a crowd of hungry onlookers. The owner of Johnson's since 1974 is John Stauffer. In the 1950s, he got his first experience in a food business when he peddled a "ding-a-ling" ice cream cart to the beach during the day and went up and down the streets of Ocean City in the evening.

At one time, there were Johnson's stores at several resort towns, but today there is only one business with three stores and a gift shop—all on Ocean City's boardwalk. Johnson's Popcorn is an icon of Ocean City, "America's Greatest Family Resort," and it is recognized not only for its quality products but for giving back to the community in so many ways.

Screaming for Ice Cream!

"I scream, you scream, we all scream for ice cream!" This familiar jingle originated as a rousing college song with silly lyrics in 1928. In the Roaring Twenties, with improved refrigeration, ice cream was popular with visitors

An ice cream vendor's horse-drawn wagon is parked right on the sand in Atlantic City, circa 1900–1910. *Courtesy of Library of Congress, Prints & Photographs, Detroit Publishing Collection.*

to beaches and boardwalks. But vacationers were screaming for ice cream long before the 1920s.

Like many foods we enjoy today, ice cream can be traced back to early civilizations, but its exact origin is unclear. The first American ice cream parlor was reportedly opened in 1776 in New York City. In 1832, an African American confectioner from Philadelphia named Augustus Jackson is credited with inventing an improved way of making ice cream, although he did not hold any patents. He also created recipes that made the product successful. Jackson worked as a chef in the White House during the 1820s and then returned to his home city and established his ice cream business.

In Victorian times, ice cream parlors were opened up in most every town across America. At the Jersey Shore, boardwalk stands and vendor wagons provided cool treats on hot summer days. Ice cream sodas and sundaes became particularly popular at pharmacies with counters and at five-and-dime stores.

Day's Ice Cream Gardens

Maintaining its Victorian allure today, Day's Ice Cream has been around since 1876 at the well-preserved Victorian seaside town of Ocean Grove, where Methodist camp meetings prevailed. Visitors can step back in time to enjoy a frosty treat while sitting at tables surrounding the courtyard garden. At one time, Day's also had stores in Morristown, Newark and Asbury Park, as well as at the Ocean Grove location.

Brothers Wilbur Fisk Day (1839–1913) and Pennington Mulford Day (1847–1928), originally from New Providence, opened a business in 1862 as "W.F. Day & Brother, Caterers, Confectioners, Ice Cream Dealers" at Morristown and Newark. In about 1882, Wilbur hired an apprentice at the Morristown store; his name was William Hershey. He became the founder of the Hershey Company in Pennsylvania, the world-famous chocolate maker.

When the Day's Ocean Grove store first opened at 48 Tilman Avenue, it was one of only two buildings on the street across from Auditorium Square. Two years later, in 1878, the Day brothers opened a second ice cream garden on Asbury Avenue. Both of these locations were seasonal summer businesses. Wilbur ran the Asbury Park store and Pennington the one in Ocean Grove. The brothers employed family members and also hired many African Americans, who were seasonal but returned year after year. Rumor has it that the great Paul Robeson was employed at the Asbury Park store and would sing while working and that variety store magnate F.W. Woolworth frequented the Ocean Grove location.

When Wilbur died in 1913, Pennington purchased the Asbury Park store from his eldest son and grandson. In 1929, just a year after Pennington died, the Asbury Park store was shut down, but his daughter, Agnes, ran the Ocean Grove location and opened the Tea Room in 1938, serving lunch and supper. In 1950, Homer K. Secor, who had worked at Day's as a young man, purchased the ice cream business from Agnes, who then devoted her time to a rooming house that she owned in Ocean Grove. "The business changed ownership several times and in 2002 began operating in conjunction with The Starving Artist Theater group."[51] The ice cream garden that is in back of the Starving Artist restaurant today looks much the same as it did in Victorian times and continues to delight ice cream lovers.

Another famous food business in the historic town of Ocean Grove that is in operation today is Nagle's Café, known for its ice cream. In Point

"Day's Ice Cream Garden, Asbury Park, N.J." This card is postmarked 1909. The shop is no longer around, but the Ocean Grove location that looks very similar is still in business.

Pleasant Beach, Hoffman's ice cream, a shore favorite, started out as a Carvel, but it was purchased by Bob Hoffman in 1956. It was closed in 2004 but was reopened under new management that same year. Although it was once part of a chain, it has been an independent ice cream shop most of the time and is known for its big sundaes that were featured on the Food Network.

The Three Kohrs

It's the biggest brand name in soft serve at the Jersey Shore. It all began back in York, Pennsylvania, in about 1919, with three young brothers of Swiss descent who delivered milk and homemade ice cream door to door. At first, they used a horse-drawn wagon, and later they upgraded to a Model T panel truck. The brothers—Archie, Clair and Elton Kohr—wanted to find a way to get ahead in business. When their uncle Sylvester Kohr told them about a new-fangled gasoline-powered machine for making soft ice cream, they were excited about the possibilities. Uncle Sylvester also urged them to take their product to the seashore. They took his advice, purchased

This great vintage photo of Kohr's Frozen Custard Inc. customers at the Farragut Avenue shop is from about 1940. The stand was destroyed by a fire and rebuilt. *Courtesy of Kohr's Frozen Custard Inc.*

a machine, lugged it to Coney Island in the summer of 1919 and set up a small booth, where they sold what they called simply "frozen dessert." In just one weekend, they sold more than eighteen thousand cones at a nickel each! To keep their product from melting too quickly in the salt air, they added eggs, which made it stiffer, and their "frozen dessert" was soon called "frozen custard." Archie Kohr, the eldest, was a schoolteacher and wasn't satisfied with the machine, so he took it all apart and redesigned it. His efforts were successful.

The story of the Kohr brothers' business enterprises becomes somewhat complicated, with conflicting versions. Elton decided to branch out on his own in 1923. Archie purchased the patent for the original machine, as well as one of his own design, but Elton's descendants contend that *he* had patented machines. The family split up in various ways and resulted in three different companies, all keeping the name Kohr in them and all making basically the same product in the same flavors and selling it at the same prices.

162

Thus, there are three distinct Kohr companies today. At the Jersey Shore, Kohr's The Original owns several stands in Seaside Heights (plus a new shop in Fairfield, New Jersey), Kohr's Frozen Custard Inc. has stands in Seaside Park and one in Seaside Heights and Kohr Bros.® (a chain with its home in Virginia and shops in thirteen states) operates its shops in Ocean City, Wildwood, North Wildwood, Cape May, Stone Harbor, Deptford and Freehold. But put any one of their famous orange and vanilla swirl cones in a child's hand, and you can be sure that he won't care which stand it came from.

Yummy Traditions

These are but some of the casual foods and eateries that were popular at the Jersey Shore before the 1960s. Many of them are well loved today. There are more too numerous to elaborate on in one small book. Cotton candy, Belgian waffles with ice cream, Italian ice, pretzels, elephant ears (a pastry popular on LBI), cheese steaks and scrapple (a fried pork mush from the Pennsylvania Dutch) are but a few of these foods. It's hard to imagine what the boardwalks would be like without food concessions. Take away the eats, and you'd have games, rides and souvenir shops, but most people enjoy fun food as part of their entertainment.

Many of the informal foods we eat have become American traditions. Food sales are an important part of the economy of the shore resorts. Could we replace them with healthy snacks? Perhaps that would be a good idea, but it probably wouldn't work. In recent years, many of the companies and stores making boardwalk treats have gone out of their way to use pure ingredients and unsaturated fats, and many do offer alternatives that are lower in calories, low in salt or sugar free.

Of course, you can bring your own snacks along if you wish. You are free to choose. No matter what you decide to eat, relaxing and having a good time is what a day at a Jersey Shore boardwalk or beach is all about. It always has been, and hopefully it always will be.

Funnel Cakes

There's no real substitute for treats purchased on the boardwalks, but perhaps on some rainy day, you'd like to try making something yummy and reminiscent of the Jersey Shore. Funnel cakes, originally a Pennsylvania Dutch delight, are fun to make. The batter is dripped into hot oil from a funnel, thus giving them their name.

2 eggs
1½ cups milk
2 tablespoons sugar
½ teaspoon salt
2 cups unbleached flour
1 teaspoon baking powder
3–4 cups cooking oil
6 tablespoons confectioners' sugar

Beat the eggs in a medium bowl. Add the milk and sugar and mix well. Combine the salt, flour and baking powder. Add this to the milk mixture. Beat with a whisk until smooth.

Add enough oil to an electric skillet so there is an inch in the pan. Heat the oil to 360 degrees F. Using a funnel with a ⅜- to ½-inch hole, put your index finger over the bottom of the funnel, allowing the batter to run slowly into the hot oil. Slowly move the funnel in circles larger and larger to make a circular pattern. The cake will be about 8 inches in diameter when done.

Fry until golden brown on one side, and then turn and fry the other side. Remove the funnel cake to a paper towel–lined plate. Drain a few minutes.

Add sugar to a sifter or strainer and shake over the funnel cake. Yields 6 funnel cakes.

From Wildwood By-the-Sea, Nostalgia & Recipes. *Courtesy of Anita S. Hirsch.*

Conclusion

The gastronomy along the 127-mile New Jersey coast is ever-changing, but many old favorites are simply reinvented. The iconic Jersey Shore foods such as seafood, pizza, pork roll and salt water taffy still rule, but the past few decades have brought new trends.

Farms have diminished in the state's coastal areas, especially in Monmouth and Ocean Counties. Housing, malls and office complexes have taken over what was once fertile soil, and yet the open land that survives is being rediscovered by a new breed of farmers who use traditional methods concurrently with modern technology.

There are an increasing number of organic farms and products. Vegetarian restaurants and veggie options are on menus at the Jersey Shore these days. They offer shore dinners such as tasty "crab" cakes made with tofu. When the Cinnamon Snail, a vegan food truck, rolls into the Red Bank Farmers' Market, people line up to order the delicious specials, and many of these customers are not even vegan.

Internationally known celebrity chef David Burke, owner of a number of restaurants including the Fromagerie in Rumson, New Jersey, worked his way up from being a dishwasher in a Route 35 motel kitchen. He uses local fish and produce in his recipes. He recently was quoted in the April 2012 *Journal*, "We have a great bounty here in this state and it's getting the recognition through locally-sourced options and using what's in season." (Chef Burke was the keynote speaker at the Monmouth County Library's "Food for Thought" program at Headquarters in Manalapan on March 4, 2012.)

Although this book focuses on the century from the mid-1800s through the mid-1900s, food history is being made all the time. A Jersey Shore restaurateur who will surely be included in future food history books is Tim McLoone. He's a superstar of the culinary scene, with seven restaurants. Known as a Renaissance man, McLoone is not only a mastermind at running restaurants, but he's also a well-known musician and philanthropist who gives much back to the local communities and beyond. Another innovative and promising restaurateur is Marilyn Schlossbach, an owner of several restaurants who worked her way up from waitress to food entrepreneur and who has helped to raise the bar for Asbury Park and other communities.

Despite such an abundance of wonderful foods, hunger is a serious problem today at some towns along the Jersey coast, as it is across the nation. Not everyone can afford famous eateries much less the cost of groceries. It must be remembered that there are people who are struggling to make ends meet in this economy.

In Red Bank, the JBJ Soul Kitchen, which opened in 2011, is an innovative way to help those who cannot afford to eat out. The restaurant where "all are welcome at our table" was the vision of rock star Jon Bon Jovi and his wife, Dorothea, who live in Monmouth County. Their dedication made the project happen through the Jon Bon Jovi Soul Foundation. The concept is simple. It's a restaurant, not a soup kitchen, but there are no prices on the menu. Those who can afford to pay for their meal make a donation, and those who can't sign up to do work, and there's a variety of duties available. This gives everyone the opportunity to go out for a nice meal, and there's no stigma attached for those who can't pay. The restaurant is an attractively renovated auto body shop at 207 Monmouth Street. The food on the menu has an emphasis on local seasonal ingredients, and the restaurant even has its own vegetable and herb garden in the front yard.

The JBJ Soul Kitchen is one example of what's being done to help foster community spirit and feed the hungry. There are many fine nonprofit organizations, shore restaurateurs and owners of boardwalk concessions and food companies that are doing their part to help their communities. They are raising funds and hosting events that benefit food banks and a wide variety of charitable projects, both local and national.

Food provides both sustenance and entertainment along the Jersey coast. Shore food businesses are a boon to tourism and ultimately to the economy of the area. Resorts that flourished in the past are making comebacks, and their eateries have given them a huge boost. Asbury Park has gone through a recent "culinary renaissance," and Atlantic City is a mecca for food. Red Bank is known for its downtown restaurants and bistros. The list could go on and on. Food is necessary, but food can also be fun. All the worries about what we should or should not eat are important, but perhaps, now and then, everyone needs a treat.

I hope you found this book to be an informative and fun gastronomic journey back in time along the Jersey coast. It's a small sampling of the myriad foods associated with the region and the historic eateries. Each one of these topics could fill a whole book, and indeed some of them have. Please make use of the sources listed in the back of this text if you are curious.

Whether you live at the Jersey Shore or are vacationing, please try some of the diverse foods available. Then, take a few deep breaths of the refreshing salt air and enjoy!

Notes

VICTORIAN AND EDWARDIAN DELIGHTS

1. Wilson, *Story of the New Jersey Shore*, 22.
2. These excerpts from Fredrika Bremer's journal and more can be found in Buchholz, *Shore Chronicles*.
3. Mock turtle was even a popular commercially canned soup. In a 1916 booklet published by the Joseph Campbell Company, Camden, New Jersey, Campbell's mock turtle soup is described as "[a] most savory and inviting soup…selected calves' heads are used in this soup." People used most every part of an animal, with nothing wasted.
4. Modern chef Brian Gualtieri of Piccola Italia, Ocean, New Jersey, suggests using a paring knife and turning the potato while you cut it. The cold water will help it to curl after it is cut.
5. This was most likely Laird's Applejack, a famous maker of the apple brandy established in 1780 and still in business in Colt's Neck.
6. Ranhofer, *The Epicurean*, 1066.
7. McMahon, *So Young, So Gay*, 143.
8. Levi and Eisenberg, *Atlantic City*, 45.
9. Wilson gave a speech at a suffragette convention in Atlantic City around this time.

10. Today, this is the site of Wilson Hall, Monmouth University, West Long Branch.
11. See http://berkeley-nj.patch.com/articles/a-haunting-in-lacey.

BOUNTY FROM THE SEA

12. The sweet milk may refer to buttermilk.
13. Moss, *Twice Told Tales*, 9
14. *Daily Advertiser,* June 10, 1790, as quoted by Moss, *Twice Told Tales*, 109.
15. Hochran, "Woolley's Looks to Reel in More Customers."
16. Mariani, *America Eats Out*, 55.
17. Moss, "Oysters Were Once New Jersey's Pearls."
18. *Fisherman's Wife by Josephine Lehman Thomas*, a story that first appeared in Scribner's (1933), was published as an illustrated book (2008) and is included in *Josephine: From Washington Working Girl to Fisherman's Wife* by Buchholz (2012)—both books by Down the Shore Publishing.
19. See www.pointpleasantlobstershanty.com.
20. Telephone interview with Jack Sinn by author, March 12, 2012.

DOWN ON THE FARM

21. Ridgway's *Chicken Foot Soup & Other Recipes* has these recipes.
22. Be sure to steam the berries using a double boiler so they don't get mushy. The meringue in her recipe is scanty; I prefer to double the amount of egg whites, but that is, of course, a matter of personal preference.
23. Uva, "Taming the Wild Beach Plum."
24. See http://www.cmcbeachplum.com for recipes.
25. See http://www.twp.howell.nj.us/content/8260/default.aspx.
26. Information from a complimentary brochure and map of Beach Plum Farm available at the Virginia Hotel.

Prohibition, the Depression and Beyond

27. Food Timeline website, "The Roaring Twenties Ice Cream Challenge," www.foodtimeline.org/sodafountain.html.
28. *Coast*, "Old Speakeasy of Allaire Village," 7–9.
29. See www.atlanticcityexperience.org.
30. In her memoir, *Growing Up in the Other Atlantic City* (2009), Turiya S.A. Raheem told what it was like to be part of her family's business, Wash's restaurant.
31. Levi and Eisenberg, *Atlantic City*, 42
32. Pike, *Asbury Park's Glory Days*, 135.
33. Richman, "Code Red."
34. *What and How: A Practical Cook Book for Every Day Living*, 27. See Food Timeline website for book information.
35. Pike, *West Long Branch*, 103.
36. Pike, *West Long Branch Revisited*, 12.
37. Charles Tomlin, *Cape May Spray*, 1913.
38. Telephone interviews with Raymond Davis were conducted by the author in the 1990s.
39. Strauss, "Mommy, Where Do Diners Come From?"
40. See http://www.cr.nps.gov/history/online_books/nj1/chap5.htm.

Casual Eats and Boardwalk Treats

41. Website for Mom's Kitchen.
42. Information about the Giunco family history is from Vic's website.
43. Telephone interview with Brockreide by Sandra Epstein, June 25, 2012.
44. *Atlantic City Sunday Press*, March 25, 1962, 12.
45. Frankie Avalon, whose hit songs included "Venus," appeared in '60s beach movies with Annette Funicello. Today, he promotes Avallone canned Jersey tomatoes, a business founded in 2010 by his sister, Theresa, and her husband, Stephen Belfiore, based in Cherry Hill, New Jersey. Their mother's picture is featured on the can label. http://www.avallonetomatoes.com.

46. *Atlantic City Sunday Press*, March 25, 1962, 12.
47. Telephone interview by author with Peter Cancro, president and founder of Jersey Mike's, June 19, 2012.
48. Obituary, *Asbury Park Press*, July 6, 2012.
49. Mullen, "It's Doggone Strange."
50. Thanks to Irving Granoff's daughter, Sandra Epstein, and her family for sharing their memories of this luncheonette.
51. The Day Family Papers are archived at the Monmouth County Historical Association in Freehold, New Jersey. Also, the Ocean Grove Historical Museum, just a few doors from Day's, houses memorabilia and information about the historic ice cream business.

Selected Bibliography and Resources

BOOKS

Bishop, Anne, and Doris Simpson. *The Victorian Seaside Cookbook*. Newark, NJ: New Jersey Historical Society, 1983.

Buchholz, Margaret Thomas. *Shore Chronicles, Diaries and Travelers' Tales from the Jersey Shore, 1764–1955*. Harvey Cedars, NJ: Down the Shore Publishing, 1999.

Cunningham, John T. *This Is New Jersey from High Point to Cape May*. New Brunswick, NJ: Rutgers University Press, 1953.

Fox, Karen. *The Chalfonte*. Cape May, NJ: Exit Zero Publishing, Inc., 2011.

Genovese, Peter. *Food Lovers' Guide to New Jersey*. 2nd ed. Guilford, CT: Globe Pequot Press, 2008.

———. *New Jersey Diners*. New Brunswick, NJ: Rutgers University Press, 1996.

Hirsch, Anita S. *Wildwood By-the-Sea: Nostalgia and Recipes.* Wildwood, NJ: Holly Beach Press, 2009.

Levi, Vicki Gold, and Lee Eisenberg. *Atlantic City: 125 Years of Ocean Madness.* Berkeley, CA: Ten Speed Press, 1979.

Mariani, John. *America Eats Out: An Illustrated History of Restaurants, Taverns, Coffee Shops, Speakeasies, and Other Establishments That Have Fed Us for 350 Years.* New York: William Morrow and Company, Inc., 1991.

McMahon, William. *So Young, So Gay: Story of the Boardwalk 1870–1970.* Atlantic City, NJ: Press Publishing and William McMahon, 1970.

Moss, George H., Jr. *Twice Told Tales.* Seabright, NJ: Ploughshare Press, 2002.

Moss, George H., Jr., and Karen L. Schnitzspahn. *Victorian Summers at the Grand Hotels of Long Branch, New Jersey.* Sea Bright, NJ: Ploughshare Press, 2000.

Napoliton, Richard. *Wall Township.* Charleston, SC: Arcadia Publishing, 1999.

Pike, Helen-Chantal. *Asbury Park's Glory Days: The Story of an American Resort.* New Brunswick, NJ: Rutgers University Press, 2005.

———. *West Long Branch.* Dover, NH: Arcadia Publishing, 1996.

———. *West Long Branch Revisited.* Charleston, SC: Arcadia Publishing, 2007.

Ranhofer, Charles. *The Epicurean: A Complete Treatise of Analytical and Practical Studies on the Culinary Art.* N.p., 1920. Originally published in 1894.

Ridgway, Arlene Martin, ed. *Chicken Foot Soup & Other Recipes from the Pine Barrens.* New Brunswick, NJ: Rutgers University Press, 1980.

Salvini, Emil R. *Boardwalk Memories: Tales of the Jersey Shore.* Guilford, CT: Globe Pequot Press, 2006.

Schnitzspahn, Karen L. *Belmar.* Dover, NH: Arcadia Publishing, 1997.

Schnitzspahn, Karen L., and Sandra Epstein. *Belmar.* Vol. 2. Dover, NH: Arcadia Publishing 1999.

———. *The Roaring '20s at the Jersey Shore.* Atglen, PA: Schiffer Publishing, 2009.

Smith, Andrew F. *The Oxford Companion to American Food and Drink.* New York: Oxford University Press Inc., 2007.

———. *Souper Tomatoes: The Story of America's Favorite Food.* New Brunswick, NJ: Rutgers University Press, 2000.

Tannahill, Reay. *Food in History.* New York: Three Rivers Press, 1988.

Waltzer, Jim, and Tom Wilk. *Tales of South Jersey.* New Brunswick, NJ: Rutgers University Press, 2001.

Wilson, Harold F. *The Story of the New Jersey Shore.* Vol. 4. New Jersey Historical Series. Princeton, NJ: D. Van Nostrand Company Inc., 1964.

Wright, Jack. *Tommy's Folly, Through Fires, Hurricanes, and War: The Story of Congress Hall, Cape May, America's Oldest Seaside Hotel.* Cape May, NJ: Beach Plum Press, 2003.

Yarvin, Brian. *Farms and Foods of the Garden State.* New York: Hippocrene Books, Inc., 2005.

PERIODICALS

Asbury Park Press
Atlantic City Press
Atlantic City Weekly
Beachcomber
Bergen Record
Cape May Spray
Cape May Times

Edible Jersey
Exit Zero
Hub/Atlanticville
The Journal
Monmouth Journal
New Jersey Monthly
New York Times
Sandpaper
Star Ledger
Sun by the Sea
Two River Times

ARTICLES

Coast. "The Old Speakeasy of Allaire Village," March and April, 1989.

D'Agnese, Joseph. "In Search of...; There's a Triple Dip of These Descendants Making Frozen Custard." *New York Times*, July 9, 2000.

Gabriel, Frank. "Hunger for History?" *Atlantic City Weekly*, November 2, 2011.

Hazard, Sharon. "The Ketchup King of Shrewsbury." *Two River Times*, January 27, 2012. http://trtnj.com/news/the-ketchup-king-of-shrewsbury.

Hochran, Adam. "Woolley's Looks to Reel in More Customers with Eyes on Expansion," April 20, 2012. http://howell.patch.com/articles/howell-establishment-ready-to-leave-bigger-footprint#c.

Hoffman, Lori. "Hackney's, Captain Starns, and the Restaurants That Were." *Atlantic City Weekly*, November 10, 2010.

————. "Renault Winery's Prohibition Loophole." *Atlantic City Weekly*, November 2, 2011.

Moss, George H., Jr. "Oysters Were Once New Jersey's Pearls." *Asbury Park Press*, August 25, 1997.

Mullen, Shannon. "It's Doggone Strange These Two Haven't Met." *Asbury Park Press*, May 18, 2000.

Richman, Alan. "Code Red." *New Jersey Monthly*, posted July 11, 2011.

Schwartz, David. "In the Neighborhood: The History of White House Subs." Casino Connection, December 1, 2010. http://casinoconnectionac.com/issue/december-2010/article/in-the-neighborhood-the-history-of-white-house-subs.

Strauss, Robert. "Mommy, Where Do Diners Come From?" *New Jersey Monthly*, January 16, 2008.

Uva, Richard H. "Taming the Wild Beach Plum," *Arnoldia* 62, no. 4 (n.d.). Cornell University.

SELECTED INTERNET SOURCES

Atlantic City Memory Lane. http://iloveac.com/memory.php. This site is for Atlantic City information and for sharing memories, including discussions of foods and eateries.

Cape May County Beach Plum Association. cmcbeachplum.com.

The Food Timeline. foodtimeline.org. Edited by Lynne Olver, this site has been a major source of information about the history and customs of foods included in this book. The timeline covers information about food and recipes from ancient times to the present.

Jersey Bites. jerseybites.com.

National Park Service. "From Marsh to Farm: The Landscape Transformation of Coastal New Jersey." nps.gov/history/history/online_books/nj3.

New Jersey Department of Agriculture. state.nj.us/jerseyfresh.

New Jersey Department of Seafood. jerseyseafood.nj.gov.

New Jersey Watercolor Artist Marie Natale. marienatale.com.

Ocean Spray. oceanspray.com.

Planters Peanuts. planters.com/history.aspx.

Taste of Wildwood. tasteofwildwood.com.

Whitesbog. whitesbog.blogspot.com.

RESOURCES

Selected Websites for Jersey Shore Eateries and Food Businesses

Angelo's Fairmount Tavern. angelosfairmounttavern.com/index.html.
Bahrs Landing. bahrslanding.com.
Branches. branchescatering.com.
The Chalfonte. chalfonte.com.
The Chatterbox. chatterboxrestaurant.com.
The Circus Drive-In. circusdrivein.com/Home_Page.html.
The Dauphin Grill. dauphingrille.com.
David Burke Fromagerie. fromagerierestaurant.com.
Delicious Orchards. deliciousorchardsnj.com.
Dock's Oyster House. docksoysterhouse.com.
The Ebbitt Room (Virginia Hotel). virginiahotel.com/ebbitt.html.
The Flanders. theflandershotel.com.
Freddie's Pizza. freddiesrpizzeria.com.
The Irish Pub. theirishpub.com.
Jack Baker's Lobster Shanty. pointpleasantlobstershanty.com.

James Candy Company. jamescandy.com.

Jersey Mike's. jerseymikes.com.

Johnson's Popcorn. johnsonspopcorn.com.

Jon Bon Jovi's Soul Kitchen. jbjsoulkitchen.org.

The Knife and Fork Inn. knifeandforkinn.com.

Kohr Bros. kohrbros.com/custard.html.

Kohr's Frozen Custard Inc. kohrsfrozencustard.com.

Kohr's The Original. kohrstheoriginal.com/home.php.

Laird's Applejack (Laird and Company). lairdandcompany.com/products_
applejack.htm.

The Lincroft Inn. lincroftinn.com.

The Lobster House. thelobsterhouse.com/home.

The Lusty Lobster. bestlobster.com.

Manco & Manco's. mancospizza.com.

Maruca's Tomato Pies. marucaspizza.com.

Max's Famous Hot Dogs. MaxsFamousHotDogs.com.

McLoone's. mcloones.com/index.php.

Mom's Kitchen. momskitchen.com.

Ollie Klein's Fish Market, Waterside Café, Grill Room & Sushi Bar.
kleinsfish.com.

The Original Fudge Kitchen. fudgekitchens.com.

Pete and Elda's. peteandeldas.com.

Piccolo Italia. piccolaitalianj.com.

The Renault Winery. renaultwinery.com.

Shriver's. shrivers.com.

Sickles Market. sicklesmarket.com.

The Smithville Inn. smithvilleinn.com.

Steel's Fudge. steelsfudge.com.

Tomasello Winery. tomasellowinery.com.

Tony's Baltimore Grill. baltimoregrill.com.

Vics. vicspizza.com.

White House Subs (no official website, see Facebook).

WindMill. windmillrestaurantsusa.com.

Selected Jersey Shore Culinary Schools and Centers

Atlantic Cape Community College. atlantic.edu/aca/index.htm.

Brookdale Community College (Monmouth County). ux.brookdalecc.edu/fac/culinary/Student_Activities.htm.

Mumford's Culinary Center (Tinton Falls). mumfords.com.

Viking Cooking School at Harrah's Resort, Atlantic City. harrahsresort.com/casinos/harrahs-atlantic-city/casino-misc/viking-cooking-school-detail.html.

There are also more culinary programs at various county vocational schools and at private institutions.

Index

About the Author

For more than twenty-five years, Karen L. Schnitzspahn has been writing and researching about the history of the Jersey Shore, where she lives. Born and raised in New Jersey, she finds the Garden State to be a diverse place with a fascinating history and delicious food. Karen is the author or co-author of nine regional New Jersey books, as well as two commemorative volumes and numerous articles. She's been the recipient of awards such as the 2007 Jane G. Clayton Award for "her outstanding efforts to preserve the history of Monmouth County." Her varied interests include the history of the American theater and nineteenth-century photography. For many years, Karen worked as a professional puppeteer and designed educational children's programs.

Visit us at
www.historypress.net